UNVEILED

15 The Chambers, Vineyard
Abingdon OX14 3FE
brf.org.uk

Bible Reading Fellowship is a charity (233280)
and company limited by guarantee (301324),
registered in England and Wales

ISBN 978 1 80039 072 0
First published 2021
Reprinted 2022
10 9 8 7 6 5 4 3 2 1

The author asserts the moral right to be identified as the author of this work

Acknowledgements
Unless otherwise acknowledged, scripture quotations are taken from The New Revised Standard Version of the Bible, Anglicised edition, copyright © 1989, 1995 by the Division of Christian Education of the National Council of the Churches of Christ in the United States of America. Used by permission. All rights reserved. • Scripture quotation marked RSV is taken from The Revised Standard Version of the Bible, copyright © 1946, 1952, 1971 by the Division of Christian Education of the National Council of the Churches of Christ in the United States of America. Used by permission. All rights reserved. • Scripture quotation marked GNT is taken from the Good News Bible published by The Bible Societies/HarperCollins Publishers Ltd, UK © American Bible Society 1966, 1971, 1976, 1992, used with permission. • Scripture quotations marked NIV are taken from The Holy Bible, New International Version (Anglicised edition) copyright © 1979, 1984, 2011 by Biblica. Used by permission of Hodder & Stoughton Publishers, a Hachette UK company. All rights reserved. 'NIV' is a registered trademark of Biblica. UK trademark number 1448790. • Scripture quotation marked KJV is taken from The Authorised Version of the Bible (The King James Bible), the rights in which are vested in the Crown, reproduced by permission of the Crown's Patentee, Cambridge University Press.

Quotations are taken from The Book of Common Prayer of 1662, the rights of which are vested in the Crown in perpetuity within the United Kingdom, reproduced by permission of Cambridge University Press, Her Majesty's Printers.

Prayers by Philippa White are copyright © Philippa White and used by kind permission.

Every effort has been made to trace and contact copyright owners for material used in this resource. We apologise for any inadvertent omissions or errors, and would ask those concerned to contact us so that full acknowledgement can be made in the future.

A catalogue record for this book is available from the British Library

Printed by Gutenberg Press, Tarxien, Malta

UNVEILED

Women of the Old Testament and the choices they made

Reflections by **Clare Hayns**   Artwork by **Micah Hayns**

To Isla, Amélie, Annabelle, Eliza, our fabulous nieces/cousins.
We hope these women will be an inspiration to you.

Acknowledgements
We'd like to thank everyone who has encouraged us along the way, particularly all those who read the Lent blog in 2020 and told us they liked it. Particular thanks to John Hayns, Alannah Jeune, and Jill Hayns for their willingness to read various versions and for their helpful comments. Also a huge thank you to Philippa White for writing so many of the prayers. Finally, we'd like to thank all the wonderful women in our lives, for their love and inspiration, especially Jane, Jill, Milly, Sara, Loïs and Helen.

Contents

ᢅᢤ Prophetic women

ᢅᢤ Hesed

ɔ‿ᴑ 'Strident' women

ɔ‿ᴑ Bad girls?

✎ #ThemToo

✎ Women at work

Introduction

This book emerged out of ignorance. A few years ago I was in a shop getting some pictures framed when the shopkeeper, seeing my clerical collar, made the statement that causes church leaders to quake: 'You'll know the answer to this, as you're a vicar.' The question he asked was, 'My son's girlfriend is called Miriam, and I know she's in the Bible – but who was she?' It was a good question, but I floundered. I knew she had something to do with Moses, but not much else. Another customer came in, so I took the opportunity to hide behind the frames to google his question!

I came away determined to find out more about Miriam and also all the other women of scripture, and I set myself the challenge of writing about a Bible woman a day for the 40 days of Lent and making that into a blog. When I began I intended to use New Testament women as well, but I found there were so many fantastic women in the Old Testament that I decided to focus on them instead.

There is an assumption that women are largely ignored in the Hebrew scriptures and that when they *are* written about, they are marginal and rather two-dimensional characters: veiled in mystery, hidden away or on the fringes. This is certainly the case for some of the women, but there are many others who are central to the narrative, complex and used by God in extraordinary ways. Through these women, I found that I was able to understand parts of the Bible that had hitherto seemed shrouded. Although their world was so often controlled by men, many of these women still had choices they could make within the constraints of their patriarchal society. Sometimes these choices had an impact on just themselves and their families, and at other times they brought about the salvation or destruction of an entire community, and even changed the course of history.

Rather than arranging the stories of these women chronologically from Genesis onwards, I decided to group them around themes which emerged, such as motherhood, work, relationships and power. We shouldn't gloss over the more disturbing or tragic stories either, as these remind us that at the heart of the human condition there is suffering and pain and the need for God's redeeming love as revealed most fully through Jesus. With this in mind, I have included a reflection and prayer at the end of each chapter, which I hope will help put the stories of these women into context.

This book is not intended to be an in-depth theological study; there are many others far more qualified than I am who have done this already. My hope is that by reading the stories and enjoying Micah's beautiful images you will get to know some of these women better and find that, even though they lived centuries ago, their stories are also incredibly current. They are women with relationship struggles, sibling rivalries, financial challenges and fertility issues. They are also women with remarkable gifts, skills, faith and fortitude.

I hope that by unveiling the stories of these remarkable women and the choices they made, we might not only learn more about them but come to know more of God's abundant love for us and for all people. I have learned so much from these women and hope that you enjoy reading about them as much as I have enjoyed writing about them.

Clare

Clare Hayns

Eve: the first choice

Now the serpent was more crafty than any other wild animal that the Lord God had made. He said to the woman, 'Did God say, "You shall not eat from any tree in the garden"?' The woman said to the serpent, 'We may eat of the fruit of the trees in the garden; but God said, "You shall not eat of the fruit of the tree that is in the middle of the garden, nor shall you touch it, or you shall die."' But the serpent said to the woman, 'You will not die; for God knows that when you eat of it your eyes will be opened, and you will be like God, knowing good and evil.' So when the woman saw that the tree was good for food, and that it was a delight to the eyes, and that the tree was to be desired to make one wise, she took of its fruit and ate.

GENESIS 3:1–6a

Much of how our life turns out depends on choices, some made by others and some of those made before we were even born: the choice of our parents to get together; decisions they then made regarding our upbringing, schooling and where we lived; their expectations for us as we grew into adulthood. We make defining choices at various stages: who we share our lives with, what we focus on, how we spend our money. Of course, sometimes events occur outside of our control: a partner leaves, a child dies, a virus changes the way we live.

The story of Eve, the first woman, has at its heart a choice. We can get bogged down worrying about whether Eve was an actual person in real time or is instead a character who helps us understand something about who we are and our relationship with the creator. In this beautiful poem of creation, we hear of 'female' being created alongside 'male' in the image of God (Genesis 1:27). God sets abundant creation before them for their enjoyment. Adam and Eve were blessed and commissioned to care for it and were given the freedom to enjoy it all, with one exception. God told them, 'Of the tree of the knowledge of good and evil you shall not eat, for in the day that you eat of it you shall die' (Genesis 2:17).

Eve had a choice to make: abide by this, or follow the voice of the serpent, who tells her that if she eats, 'Your eyes will be opened, and you will be like God, knowing good and evil.' The fruit looked 'good' and 'was a delight to the eyes', and Eve made the choice to eat, sharing the fruit with Adam.

After they had eaten, Eve and Adam became fearful, blaming one another and hiding from God. The world that had been abundant, beautiful and safe now included pain, suffering and fear. This pain must have been keenly felt by Eve as she experienced brokenness within her own family, with her son Cain killing his brother Abel (Genesis 4).

Eve is so often blamed for causing 'the fall', a term not mentioned in the Bible but which describes the rupture in the relationship between humanity and God. I wonder if it's more helpful to view Eve as the first rather than the cause. She was the first to make a choice which had repercussions causing pain and a breakdown in a relationship. She was certainly not the last. Every human being at one stage or another will have made choices which have caused pain and separation. Most of us do this, to a greater or lesser extent, every day. It is part of being human – it is what is meant by sin.

Eve may have been the first woman to choose independence from God, but she was also the first to have been in relationship with God. She was the first to walk with God in the garden, to speak to God and to hear God's voice.

As the relationship between God and humankind was broken in a garden, it is perhaps no surprise that in a garden is also where it is restored. The first encounter the risen Jesus has is also in a garden, this time with a woman called Mary Magdalene, who initially mistakes him for a gardener but on hearing him call her 'Mary' recognises him as the Lord (John 20:16).

Reflection

Like Eve, each one of us has been created in the image of God and given a glorious world to inhabit. We too have choices: how we live, who we love and what we do with the gift of life we've been given. We acknowledge the choices we've made which have caused pain. And we remember that in all of the joys and pains that make up a human life, God never abandons us. God continues to walk alongside us, urging us into restored relationship, but giving us a choice to follow him or not – and loving us regardless.

Prayer

God of all creation, in whose image all human beings are made, help us to choose to live lives that radiate your love. Amen

Mum's the word

The central narrative for many of our Old Testament women is whether or not they are able to produce offspring. In a traditional society the primary role of women is childbearing, ensuring the continuation of the family or tribe. The next Old Testament women we look at remind us that mothering has never been easy. They demonstrate through their joys and sorrows the remarkable strength, faith and resilience needed to bring up children. Here we see mothers having to protect their children from violent rivals (Hagar), murderous rulers (Jochebed) and poverty (the widow of Zarephath). We are reminded that mothers are far from perfect and make mistakes (Sarah, Rebekah), and that many mothers have to face the pain of loss and grief (Hannah, Rizpah). These women were much more than just a means to produce offspring.

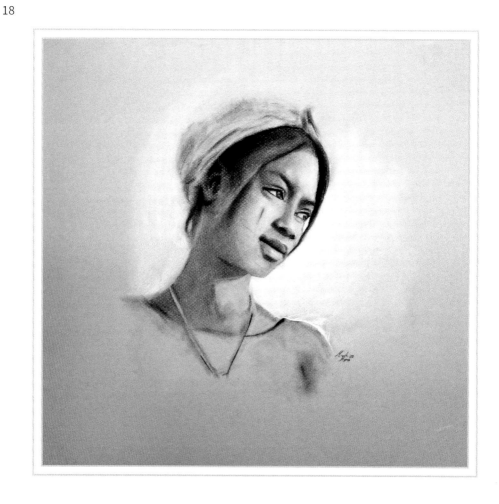

2

Hagar: seen and heard

The angel of the Lord found [Hagar] by a spring of water in the wilderness, the spring on the way to Shur. And he said, 'Hagar, slave-girl of Sarai, where have you come from and where are you going?' She said, 'I am running away from my mistress Sarai.' The angel of the Lord said to her, 'Return to your mistress, and submit to her.' The angel of the Lord also said to her, 'I will so greatly multiply your offspring that they cannot be counted for multitude.'

GENESIS 16:7–10

In Margaret Atwood's dystopian novel *The Handmaid's Tale*, the United States has become a military dictatorship and women are assigned specific roles to ensure the continuation of the revolutionary party. The novel is seen through the eyes of Offred, one of the army of handmaids whose role is to produce offspring for the powerful commanders, many of whom can't conceive with their wives. Offred is her slave name, literally meaning 'of Fred'; her true name is never revealed in the novel.

Hagar, like Offred, was also a servant of a wealthy infertile couple and her body was similarly used to conceive a child. Hagar simply means 'stranger' and she was an outsider, an Egyptian slave-girl owned by Abram's wife, Sarai. What is remarkable is that Hagar, a woman with no authority and no real name, is the only person in the whole of scripture to give God a name.

Abram and Sarai had endured years of infertility, and Sarai decided to have a child via the means of her slave as a surrogate. Abram willingly went along with the plan, and Hagar became pregnant, a status that gave her some authority. Sarai believed that Hagar 'looked with contempt' towards her and became increasingly jealous until 'she dealt harshly with her'. Hagar, fearing for the safety of her unborn child, fled into the wilderness (Genesis 16:6).

It was as she was hiding near a well that Hagar encountered 'the angel of the Lord', who spoke to her about her unborn son, Ishmael, and told her that her descendants would be so numerous 'they cannot be counted'. Hagar was so overwhelmed at having been seen and heard, perhaps for the first time in her life, that she gave the Lord a name: 'You are El-roi' (which means 'God who sees'); for she said, 'Have I really seen God?' (Genesis 16:13).

The angel told her to return to her mistress, and soon afterwards she gave birth to Ishmael, who she brought up in Sarai's household until Sarah, now with a new name, conceived and gave birth to Isaac. Once Sarah had a son of her own, she didn't want Hagar and Ishmael to inherit, and so they were banished once again. Ishmael was almost an adult by this time, around 15 years old, and the exiled pair wandered in the desert until their food and water dried up and all hope of survival had gone. In the first description of a death ritual in scripture, Hagar put her son under a bush, sat at a distance and waited for him to die.

God heard their cries once again and appeared to them, rather like the angel that appeared to Mary centuries later, saying, 'Do not be afraid; for God has heard' (Genesis 21:17). A well of water appeared, they survived and Ishmael became the father of a numerous and powerful tribe. He is revered today by Arab Muslims as their patriarch and regarded in Islam as an ancestor to the prophet Muhammad. Hagar, an enslaved outsider who was abused and mistreated by her mistress, was seen and heard by God.

Reflection

We need to have our eyes open to the hard fact that slavery has been and continues to be part of the culture of our world. Margaret Atwood's Gilead may not exist, but her imagined land is not far from the reality of so many women, and the presumption of ownership and sexual rights over another person is sadly not something confined to history or fiction. Over 40 million people, most of them women, are estimated to be held against their will today. Let us pray that they, like Hagar, are seen and heard by God.

Prayer

El-roi, the God who sees and hears all those who cry out in need, bring comfort and freedom to all your children, especially those who are oppressed, who live in fear of violence and who are forced to flee their homes to protect their families. Amen

3

Sarah: under the oaks

The Lord appeared to Abraham by the oaks of Mamre, as he sat at the entrance of his tent in the heat of the day. He looked up and saw three men standing near him. When he saw them, he ran from the tent entrance to meet them, and bowed down to the ground. He said, 'My lord, if I find favour with you, do not pass by your servant'... They said to him, 'Where is your wife Sarah?' And he said, 'There, in the tent.' Then one said, 'I will surely return to you in due season, and your wife Sarah shall have a son.' And Sarah was listening at the tent entrance behind him.

GENESIS 18:1–3, 9–10

I have always loved trees. As a child growing up in Buckinghamshire, we had a huge sycamore tree in our garden which we, not very imaginatively, called 'The Big Tree'. It was said to be one of the largest and oldest of its kind in the UK and was simply magnificent. One branch came right to the ground, perfect for climbing up into a cavity in the middle. It was the place we went to as children to get away from everyone. My first experience of prayer was here, as I spoke to God about whatever problems I was having, usually some kind of sibling rivalry or another. The story of Sarai (her name is later changed to Sarah) features a particular tree, or group of trees, evocatively named 'the oaks of Mamre'.

Sarai was married to Abram (later called Abraham), who was her half-brother. They spent much of their life travelling, as Abram had been called by God to leave their homeland, Haran, and go into a new land where, the Lord told him, they would be blessed (Genesis 12:1–3). They were indeed blessed in many ways, with wealth, land and livestock. But not with a child – all that Sarai really wanted and all that was expected of her as a woman. The very first thing we learn about her is that she 'was barren; she had no child' (Genesis 11:30).

It was near the oaks of Mamre that two incidents occurred which changed the course of Sarai's life. It was here that Abram first received the promise that they would have a child and that their offspring would be so numerous they would be 'like the dust of the earth' (Genesis 13:16). And it was also at the foot of the oaks of Mamre many years later when Sarah and Abraham had another encounter with the Lord, who came to them in the guise of three strangers. Again they were given a promise, that by the following year they would have a son.

Sarah laughed at the prospect. She was now past the menopause or, as the Bible delicately puts it, 'It had ceased to be with [her] after the manner of women.' Abraham was also past his prime: 'My husband is old, shall I have pleasure?' (Genesis 18:11–12).

But this time, the promise *was* fulfilled and Sarah did indeed have a child, Isaac (which means 'he laughs'). Sarah's life can't have been easy. She had no choice but to follow her husband in his travels, and Abraham twice asked her to deny she was his wife so she could sleep with men in authority to protect his own life. As we will see in the next chapter on Hagar, Sarah struggled with jealousy and behaved appallingly towards her slave girl. But she was also faithful and robust and is remembered in all three Abrahamic faiths as one of the few biblical matriarchs.

At the end of her long life, in the first description of a funeral and burial in scripture, Sarah was buried in a place lovingly secured by her husband Abraham, and where he would later join her: in a plot overlooking her beloved oaks of Mamre.

Reflection

The Bible has many stories of people meeting with God while sitting near trees. I think of Jonah, who sulked under a bush, and of Jesus' encounter with Nathaniel: 'I saw you under the fig tree' (John 1:48). The Big Tree was the first place I can remember encountering the divine, and since then I have often enjoyed sitting and praying at the foot of trees. Perhaps they remind us of God's permanence and stability, especially comforting in times of change and uncertainty.

Prayer

Heavenly Father, thank you that you see us and hear us when we come to you in prayer. As you heard your daughter Sarah many centuries ago, we pray that you would hear us today as we speak to you of all that we long for. Amen

4

Rebekah:
faith and favouritism

And Rebekah looked up, and when she saw Isaac, she slipped quickly from the camel, and said to the servant, 'Who is the man over there, walking in the field to meet us?' The servant said, 'It is my master.' So she took her veil and covered herself. And the servant told Isaac all the things that he had done. Then Isaac brought her into his mother Sarah's tent. He took Rebekah, and she became his wife; and he loved her.

GENESIS 24:64–67a

'Behold, Rebekah.'

GENESIS 24:51 (RSV)

We first meet Rebekah with a jar on her shoulder as she goes to a well outside the town gates to draw water. She is the first of several women in the Bible whose story entails leaving their home to marry a suitor they've not yet met. It is a story that involves camels, nose rings, a family feud and troublesome twins.

Abraham was by now an elderly patriarch and wanted to find a wife for his son Isaac from his own home country, rather than from Canaan where they now lived. His estate manager, Eliezer, was sent on a quest to Nahor (in modern-day Syria) to find someone suitable from Abraham's clan. He took with him camels laden with bags of jewels as a dowry and went to the place where the women were most likely to be seen, the town well, and there he prayed for guidance.

Rebekah was both beautiful and wealthy, the daughter of Bethuel, Abraham's nephew, and sister of Laban. We are told she had a nurse, Deborah, and several maids.

She arrived at the well before Eliezer had finished praying. When she offered to fetch water for him and his camels, he took this as a sign from the Lord and gave her gifts of a nose ring and two gold arm bracelets. In a further display of generosity, she invited him back to her father's house where, after some negotiation over lavish hospitality and more gifts (jewels, gold and cloth), the family concluded that the Lord did indeed intend for Rebekah to marry Isaac. Rebekah was asked if she was willing to leave her home to go to a foreign land to marry a stranger, and she gave her consent with a simple answer: 'I will' (Genesis 24:58).

She married Isaac and eventually, after a difficult pregnancy, gave birth to twin boys, Esau and Jacob. Her boys were very different from each other, Esau being a rugged hunter and Jacob a quieter, more reflective type. Family dynamics are rarely straightforward, and often jealousies, feuds and rivalries are formed early on. This family was no exception, and perhaps it began here: 'Isaac loved Esau… but Rebekah loved Jacob' (Genesis 25:28).

The family rift grew when Rebekah disapproved of Esau's choice of wives and then plotted to make sure that Jacob would gain his father's blessing over and above his older twin. This plot led to Jacob receiving his brothers' rightful blessing, and it also precipitated a fraternal feud which lasted many years and meant that Rebekah's favourite son had to flee into exile to her brother Laban.

We don't know if Rebekah lived long enough to see her beloved son again, or if she ever saw his eventual reconciliation with his brother. The last we hear of her is that she was buried alongside Isaac, Abraham and Sarah in the family tomb near the oaks of Mamre.

Reflection

Rebekah was a courageous and bold woman of God, not afraid to take risks, to speak her mind and to use the power she had to secure what she wanted for those she loved. Her actions caused conflict within her family, though, and her sons' rivalry was perhaps partly due to their parents' favouritism. Recent research conducted in the UK found that 30% of people thought their parents had a favourite child and believed this had had a lasting impact on family relations.

Parenting isn't easy, and so let's pray for all those who navigate this tricky path, and who get it wrong at times; and for ourselves that we wouldn't let old wounds fester.

Prayer

God of love, through Jesus Christ you draw us into one great family of disciples: help us to see others as you see them. Forgive us when our actions cause hurt and division, and help us to love those whom we find difficult. Amen

5

Jochebed: the secret mother

> Now a man from the house of Levi went and married a Levite woman. The woman conceived and bore a son; and when she saw that he was a fine baby, she hid him for three months. When she could hide him no longer she got a papyrus basket for him, and plastered it with bitumen and pitch; she put the child in it and placed it among the reeds on the bank of the river. His sister stood at a distance, to see what would happen to him.
>
> EXODUS 2:1–4

Moses is the most important prophet in Judaism and one of the most significant in Christianity and Islam. He led the Israelites out of Egyptian captivity, he was given the ten commandments, thereby establishing Jewish law, and he is believed to have been the author of the Torah, the first five books of the Bible. However, without the bravery of several women he may never have made it beyond the first few months of life. We will hear in a later chapter about the courage of the Israelite midwives in preventing infanticide; here we learn of how his mother, sister and an Egyptian princess came together in an extraordinary way to protect his life.

Having a baby during a time of war or persecution is a terrifying ordeal, one that millions of women endure every year. The situation was dire. Pharaoh had issued an edict to murder all the Hebrew baby boys by throwing them into the River Nile, and Jochebed had given birth to 'a fine baby' at this dangerous time.

Jochebed was one of Levi's daughters, and therefore was one of Jacob's grand-children. She was married to Amram and had two older children, Aaron and Miriam. She had successfully hidden her newborn baby for three months, but this was becoming impossible to sustain. She needed another plan. So she created a basket out of reeds and waterproofed it with a plant resin. Then she took the 'moses basket' and hid it near where the wealthy women bathed in the river. Her daughter Miriam was stationed to watch over the baby, and I imagine both mother and daughter prayed earnestly to God for his protection. They could not have imagined in their wildest dreams that his salvation would come from the very place that also posed the greatest risk to his life.

Pharaoh's daughter Bithiah was bathing in the river alongside her entourage and spotted the baby in the reeds. If she had followed her father's rules, she would have been obliged to hand him over to the authorities. What she did was far more risky. Realising he was a Hebrew baby, she took pity on him and decided to adopt him. He was still breastfeeding and, in an extraordinary twist and an answer to Jochebed's prayers, Miriam, who had been watching all this unfold, stepped forward and offered to find a wet nurse for the baby. So Moses' own mother was paid to look after her child until adulthood, presumably from the safety of the royal palace or its surroundings.

Reflection

We can imagine Jochebed's joy at the return of her beautiful son, and the delight that they could now live in safety, without fear. Her story reminds us of Mary who, over a thousand years later, also had to flee a despotic ruler, Herod, to protect her newborn son Jesus. Women throughout the world make sacrifices each and every day to ensure their children thrive. Many of these acts are unremarkable and go by unnoticed, such as those who take two jobs or who put their careers on hold for a time. Sometimes the sacrifice is particularly costly. While working for a homeless charity, I remember meeting a woman who had offered up her child for adoption as she knew she wouldn't have been able to look after him. Her decision was painful and was clearly made out of a deep love for her little boy. This story also reminds us that the care of children is so often done by a community working together, and so we think of all the foster parents, respite carers, nannies and siblings who so often take on these caring roles to help children thrive.

Prayer

God of Miriam and Jochebed,
you care for those the world forgets
and you never forget the needs of your people.
Be present with all who make agonising decisions;
protect children who have nobody to protect them;
bless those who foster, adopt and take care of children;
and may all the members of your family
live for one another in self-giving love.
Philippa White

6

Hannah: she rose

As [Hannah] continued praying before the Lord, Eli observed her mouth. Hannah was praying silently; only her lips moved, but her voice was not heard; therefore Eli thought she was drunk. So Eli said to her, 'How long will you make a drunken spectacle of yourself? Put away your wine.' But Hannah answered, 'No, my lord, I am a woman deeply troubled; I have drunk neither wine nor strong drink, but I have been pouring out my soul before the Lord.'

1 SAMUEL 1:12–15

There are several women in scripture whose narrative revolves around infertility and the deep longing for a child. In a patriarchal society, to be married and childless was the gravest social disgrace, one that was generally blamed on the woman in the partnership. The pressure to conceive, as we will see in Hannah's story, didn't always come from the man. It often came from the women around them, who could be unbearably cruel. Childless women were often pitied, shunned by their peers and excluded from society.

Hannah lived in Israel at the time when Eli was the high priest. She was married to Elkanah, who, as the society was polygamous, had a second wife called Peninnah. Their situation is summed up in 1 Samuel 1:2: 'Peninnah had children, but Hannah had no children.' Peninnah was unkind; she 'used to provoke her severely, to irritate her, because the Lord had closed her womb' (1 Samuel 1:6). This went on 'year after year', especially whenever Hannah went to worship. Hannah became depressed, and 'wept and would not eat' (1 Samuel 1:7).

Bullying someone to the point that their mental health and well-being deteriorates to that extent would now be considered harassment. Elkanah seems to have been supportive but missed the point entirely. He gave her double portions of food 'because he loved her', but he was oblivious to the real reasons for Hannah's pain: 'Hannah, why do you weep? Why do you not eat? Why is your heart sad? Am I not more to you than ten sons?' (1 Samuel 1:8).

The turning point in Hannah's story comes with two powerful words: 'Hannah rose' (1 Samuel 1:9). Despite her sadness, and the fact she was tormented by Peninnah each time she went, Hannah managed to muster the strength to rise up and go to the temple to pray. One day she was pouring out her soul so earnestly and with such passion that Eli, the temple priest, thought she must be drunk! She vowed that if God gave her a child, she would repay this blessing by offering him back to the Lord to live and work in the temple. Her prayers were answered, and she carried out her promise to the Lord. When her child, Samuel (which means 'God has heard'), was fully weaned, probably about three years old, she took him to the temple where he grew up under Eli's guidance. Hannah visited him every year with clothes she had lovingly made for him, and went on to have five more children.

Samuel grew up to be one of the greatest prophets in Israel.

Reflection

> But we have this treasure in clay jars, so that it may be made clear that this extraordinary power belongs to God and does not come from us. We are afflicted in every way, but not crushed; perplexed, but not driven to despair.
> 2 CORINTHIANS 4:7–8

There are times in life when everything and everyone seems to be against us, our prayers remain unanswered and, like Hannah, our hearts are sad. This can be even more difficult when those closest to us are unkind and cruel, and when others just don't get it. Anyone who has lived through depression or mental ill-health will connect with the frustration Hannah must have felt with poor Elkanah's hopeless attempts at support: 'Why are you sad? Am I not enough?' Turning to prayer in these dark times is hard to do, but Hannah mustered the strength to rise up and be honest with God, even at the risk of looking a fool as she did so. Let us pray for those battling with depression and take heart from the promise in 2 Corinthians 4 that we will not be crushed or driven to despair.

Prayer

Almighty and everlasting God,
the comfort of the sad and strength of those who suffer;
let the prayers of your children who cry out of any tribulation
   come to you;
and to every soul that is distressed
grant mercy, grant relief, grant refreshment;
through Jesus Christ our Lord. Amen
The Book of Common Prayer

7

Rizpah: she kept watch

The seven of them perished together. They were put to death in the first days of harvest, at the beginning of the barley harvest. Then Rizpah the daughter of Aiah took sackcloth, and spread it on a rock for herself, from the beginning of harvest until rain fell on them from the heavens; she did not allow the birds of the air to come on the bodies by day, or the wild animals by night.

2 SAMUEL 2:9b–10

A few years ago, we visited some World War I burial sites. Seeing the miles of identical gravestones marking the loss of so many young lives moved me to tears. There can be nothing more painful for a parent than the death of a child. The story of Rizpah is not for the faint-hearted. It is a story of a woman caught in the midst of a bloody war. There are great stretches of the Old Testament that document a seemingly endless number of wars and battles, with some truly gruesome stories of torture and retribution.

Rizpah exemplifies the love of a mother who, even in the most distressing of circumstances, refused to allow her sons to be dishonoured in their death. In ancient Israel a decent burial was considered to be a sign of God's blessing, while being left out in the open after death was a curse for disobeying the covenant: 'Your corpses shall be food for every bird of the air and animal of the earth, and there shall be no one to frighten them away' (Deuteronomy 28:26).

Rizpah was one of King Saul's concubines, and she had two sons. After Saul's death, Rizpah was pursued by Abner, Saul's commander-in-chief. We don't know what really happened, but all we hear is that Saul's son Ishbaal accused Abner of sleeping with her in a bid to seize power. Abner was furious enough to change allegiance. He joined David, who was by then becoming increasingly powerful.

A long war ensued between the two houses of Saul and David, and then famine struck the battle-torn region. Ancient cultures often believed natural disaster to be a sign of the Lord's displeasure. David heard from the Lord that the famine was because, many years before, Saul had broken an oath made with the Gibeonite tribe. David wanted to make amends and so asked the Gibeonites what they required. They, seeking revenge, demanded the deaths of seven of Saul's sons. David duly handed over Rizpah's sons, alongside five of Saul's grandsons, and 'they impaled them on the mountain before the Lord' (2 Samuel 21:9). In a further act of humiliation, their bodies were left hanging where they died.

We can only imagine the grief of the mothers of these men as they witnessed the brutal deaths and were prevented from carrying out the burial rituals. Rizpah didn't leave the bodies and set up vigil on a rock nearby. She prevented the bodies from being desecrated and, for around six months, 'did not allow the birds of the air to come on the bodies by day, or the wild animals by night'.

Her constant presence must have caused a stir because David eventually heard about her vigil and had a change of heart. He had the bodies removed and they were buried alongside the bodies of Saul and Jonathan in a family tomb. It was only then that the long days of famine came to an end.

Reflection

Meanwhile, standing near the cross of Jesus were his mother, and his mother's sister, Mary the wife of Clopas, and Mary Magdalene.
JOHN 19:25

Rizpah's story reminds us of another mother who stood and watched while her innocent son died. Mary, like Rizpah before her, didn't have any power to change the course of events that led to her son being hung on a tree. All that these women could do was stand nearby and watch as the worst happened. But their choice to remain and not run from suffering is a powerful one, and a choice that women make every day as they sit by the bedside of sick children, visit their children in prison and prepare their children for burial. Let us pray for all those who 'stand near', even when to do so must be unbearably painful.

Prayer

Watch, O Lord, with those who wake, or watch, or weep tonight,
and give your angels and saints charge over those who sleep.
Tend your sick ones, O Lord Christ.
Rest your weary ones, soothe your suffering ones,
pity your afflicted ones, shield your joyous ones,
and all for your love's sake. Amen
Augustine of Hippo (354–430)

8

The widow of Zarephath: giving and receiving

> hen the word of the Lord came to [Elijah], saying, 'Go now to Zarephath, which belongs to Sidon, and live there; for I have commanded a widow there to feed you.' So he set out and went to Zarephath. When he came to the gate of the town, a widow was there gathering sticks; he called to her and said, 'Bring me a little water in a vessel, so that I may drink.'
>
> 1 KINGS 17:8–10

I help out at our local food bank, which provides much-needed sustenance to an ever-growing number of people who struggle to provide food for their families. Emily is one of the most regular volunteers, and she was herself a recipient of the food bank just a year ago. Her husband had left her to look after her five children on her own, she lost her job and she struggled to make ends meet. She was determined that she would help others in her position as soon as she could, and she has been true to her word.

In this story we meet a widow and a prophet, both hungry and in need, who helped each other in a most extraordinary way. The 'widow of Zarephath' was left on her own to care for a young child after her husband died. The king of Israel at the time was Ahab, 'who did evil in the sight of the Lord' (1 Kings 16:30). The prophet Elijah had predicted that Ahab's disobedience would lead to a time of drought, and this prediction came true. The once-flourishing region was suffering, food was scarce and the most vulnerable, like this widow, were struggling to survive. During the drought Elijah had been eking out a meagre existence on the banks of a stream, being fed by ravens. However, when the wadi eventually dried up, Elijah needed help and so followed God's guidance to Zarephath.

The hungry pair met at the city gates where the widow was gathering sticks for what she believed would be her final meal with her son before they starved. The parched prophet asked her for water, which she provided, but then he asked for more: 'Bring me a morsel of bread in your hand' (1 Kings 17:11). It may only have been a morsel, but even that meagre amount was too much for her: 'I have nothing baked, only a handful of meal in a jar, and a little oil in a jug' (1 Kings 17:12).

Elijah's reaction to hearing of her poverty was surprising. He told her to go home to prepare her final meal, but before doing this he asked her to use the little flour and oil she had left to make some bread for him. He promised that there would be enough, not just for that day but until the drought ended. The widow did as she was asked and 'her household ate for many days. The jar of meal was not emptied, neither did the jug of oil fail' (1 Kings 17:15–16).

The widow's story doesn't end there, though, because tragedy struck and her beloved son became ill and died. She cried out to Elijah, who was by then her lodger: 'What have you against me, O man of God?' (1 Kings 17:18). Elijah had no words to answer her, only actions. He took hold of her son, carried him to an upper room, cried to the Lord and, in a remarkable act of faith, 'stretched himself upon on the child' and prayed. His prayers were answered and the boy lived: 'See, your son is alive' (1 Kings 17:23).

Reflection

There are many echoes between this story of the widow and Elijah and Jesus' teachings and miracles, but I am also reminded of the widow who put all her coins into the temple collection plate. Jesus said of her, 'Truly I tell you, this poor widow has put in more than all of them; for all of them have contributed out of their abundance, but she out of her poverty has put in all she had to live on' (Luke 21:3–4).

The manager of the food bank tells me that poorer churches and communities are often the most generous in their food donations. The worst days of the Covid pandemic felt rather like a time of drought when we thirsted for human interaction and for the things that nourish us. Many people struggled to feed their families, and it is still the poor who are suffering the most. Perhaps this story is a reminder to us all to be generous with what we have, and we might also pray that God would transform what we can offer into abundant blessings for others.

Prayer

Dearest Lord, teach me to be generous;
teach me to serve thee as thou deserves;
to give and not count the cost,
to fight and not heed the wounds,
to toil and not to seek for rest,
to labour and not to seek reward,
save that of knowing that I do your will.
St Ignatius of Loyola (1491–1556)

Prophetic women

A prophet is a man or woman who has been called by God to speak on God's behalf. The Hebrew word for prophet is *nabi* (male) or *nebiah* (female), which comes from *naba*, meaning 'call'. We are far more familiar with the male *nabi* in the Old Testament, such as Moses, Isaiah and Jeremiah. Although there are only a few prophetic women mentioned in the Hebrew scriptures, the text doesn't indicate they were particularly unusual, so there may well have been others whose stories haven't survived. Miriam, Deborah and Huldah have very different gifts, but they reveal that God has been speaking through women for many centuries.

54

9

Miriam: the joyful prophet

When the horses of Pharaoh with his chariots and his chariot drivers went into the sea, the Lord brought back the waters of the sea upon them; but the Israelites walked through the sea on dry ground. Then the prophet Miriam, Aaron's sister, took a tambourine in her hand; and all the women went out after her with tambourines and with dancing. And Miriam sang to them: 'Sing to the Lord, for he has triumphed gloriously; horse and rider he has thrown into the sea.'

EXODUS 15:19–21

In May 2020 a man named Archie Williams went on *America's Got Talent* and told his powerful story. He had recently been released after serving 37 years in Angola State Penitentiary, one of the harshest prisons in Louisiana, where he had been incarcerated for a rape and attempted murder that he did not commit. There had been no evidence placing him at the scene of the crime, but as a poor black man he wasn't able to fight the justice system. After decades in prison his innocence was proved through a re-examination of the DNA evidence. He told the hushed crowd that his way of surviving was through prayer and through singing.

There is enormous power in song, as testified by oppressed peoples throughout the ages, and so it is not surprising that the first thing that the Israelites do when they reach their freedom is to sing. It is perhaps more surprising to hear that the first worship leader mentioned in the Bible is a woman. Miriam was the older sister of Moses. It is likely that she was the one who had watched over him as a vulnerable baby in the bulrushes and secured his safety.

One of the defining narratives of the Judeo-Christian faith is the exodus, the story of how God led his people out of captivity and into freedom. It's repeated in many different ways throughout scripture, from the release of the Israelites enslaved in Egypt under the Pharaohs, to the liberation from persecution in the time of Esther and to freedom for all people through Jesus Christ. Moses was called by God, alongside his brother Aaron, to confront Pharaoh and ask for freedom for the Israelites (Exodus 3:1–10). It took ten plagues for the Egyptian ruler to relent, and even then he changed his mind and pursued them as they escaped across the Red Sea. The Israelites reached freedom when the water miraculously parted, allowing them to escape, and their pursuers were destroyed in the churning sea.

When they reached land, they sang a song of triumph and liberation, and the women were led in worship by 'the prophet Miriam', who 'took a tambourine in her hand' and 'sang to them'. It is remarkable that when they fled Egypt, when they didn't even have time to wait for their bread to rise, they remembered to take their musical instruments. It's as if they knew there would be a time to celebrate again one day, and they made sure they were ready.

Miriam died during a drought in the wilderness of Zin, and she was remembered many years later by the prophet Micah as one of the three great prophets (with Moses and Aaron) who were sent by God to deliver his people from captivity.

Reflection

I was struck by the role played by song during the global Covid-19 pandemic. For many people of faith, the restriction on congregational singing was one of the most painful losses to bear. This was perhaps because we know how important it is to join our voices together in praise and worship in times of anxiety and suffering. For this reason, it is not surprising that music became such a balm for many, and the priestly blessing uttered by Aaron, Miriam's brother, became an anthem of the time. His words were put to music and sung by 'virtual choirs' throughout the world:

> The Lord bless you and keep you;
> the Lord make his face to shine upon you, and be gracious to you;
> the Lord lift up his countenance upon you, and give you peace.
> NUMBERS 6:24–26

Let us be thankful for musicians and all those who lead us in worship and praise, particularly during times of hardship.

Prayer

O God, whom saints and angels delight to worship in heaven:
Be ever present with your servants who seek through art and music
to perfect the praises offered by your people on earth;
and grant to them even now glimpses of your beauty,
and make them worthy at length to behold it unveiled
for evermore; through Jesus Christ our Lord. Amen

Prayer for Church Musicians and Artists,
The Book of Common Prayer

✦ 10 ✦

Deborah: the warrior judge

At that time Deborah, a prophetess, wife of Lappidoth, was judging Israel. She used to sit under the palm of Deborah between Ramah and Bethel in the hill country of Ephraim; and the Israelites came up to her for judgement. She sent and summoned Barak son of Abinoam from Kedesh in Naphtali, and said to him, 'The Lord, the God of Israel, commands you, "Go, take position at Mount Tabor, bringing ten thousand from the tribe of Naphtali and the tribe of Zebulun. I will draw out Sisera, the general of Jabin's army, to meet you by the Wadi Kishon with his chariots and his troops; and I will give him into your hand."' Barak said to her, 'If you will go with me, I will go; but if you will not go with me, I will not go.'

JUDGES 4:4–8

In December 1919, Ada Jane Summers became the first British woman to preside over a trial as a magistrate. Much has changed since then, and women now make up over half of all magistrates, but they are still significantly underrepresented in the judiciary, not just in the UK but also globally. Lady Brenda Hale, one of the top judges in the UK, has been a powerful advocate for better gender representation in the profession. In a speech marking the centenary of women in law, she recalled a ruling in the US which barred women from certain occupations. It stated that the 'natural and proper timidity and delicacy which belongs to the female sex evidently unfits it for many of the occupations of civil life'.[1]

The author of that ruling had clearly not read about Deborah, the only female judge mentioned in the Bible. Deborah was remarkable. Not only was she the first recorded prophet – male or female – in Israel since the time of Moses, but she was also the only woman that we know of to be called by God into a position of civil authority in Israel. Her role as judge was to hold court 'under the palm of Deborah', where she would mediate disputes, give strategic advice in conflicts and impart God's will to the community. She was a wise leader, and her brilliant strategic mind helped to win an important battle against Israel's enemies.

The people of Israel were now a loosely organised group of tribes who were learning how to live in a settled way under God's covenant. The book of Judges chronicles a cycle of rebellion and deliverance which follows this basic pattern: the people are unfaithful and turn to worshipping other gods; God becomes angry and hands them over to their enemies who oppress them; the people cry out for mercy, which God sends in the form of an inspired 'judge' who rescues them; they return to normal life for a while and then forget about God and start worshipping Baal or other gods again, and the cycle repeats.

The story of Deborah follows this pattern. Israel had rebelled against God and had been oppressed for 20 years by Jabin, the king of the Canaanites. A battle had broken out. Jabin's army was led by a powerful general called Sisera, who commanded professional warriors and chariots. The Israelite army, led by Barak, was far weaker; they seemed likely to lose and so cried out to the Lord for help. Deborah's plan was that the Israelites should occupy Mount Tabor, high above Sisera's base. She told them that God had heard their cries and this was his divine plan to rescue them, and Barak agreed on the condition that she went with him.

Deborah assented to Barak's request and accompanied him into the battle, but not before warning him that it would always be known that 'the Lord will sell Sisera into the hand of a woman' (Judges 4:9). Deborah's strategy was successful. Flash floods wiped out Sisera's chariots, giving the Israelites, who had been safe in the hills, a tactical advantage. It was a resounding victory for God's people: 'All the army of Sisera fell by the sword; no one was left' (Judges 4:16). Sisera alone was spared. He left the battle on foot and ran to what he believed was safe territory, where he met Jael, another woman who proved that 'timidity and delicacy' are not qualities that always belong to the female sex!

Reflection

The Advisory Panel on Judicial Diversity (2010) found that 'in a democratic society, the judiciary should reflect the diversity of society'.[2] Women like Ada Jane Summers and Lady Brenda Hale have been trailblazers for women in the judiciary. Perhaps they were inspired by Deborah before them. It is not easy being a minority in any profession, and so we give thanks for those who forge a path for others to follow.

Prayer

O God of righteousness, lead us, we pray, in the ways of justice and peace: inspire us to break down all oppression and wrong, to gain for everyone their due reward, and from everyone their due service, that each may live for all, and all may care for each, in the name of Jesus Christ our Lord. Amen

Archbishop William Temple (1881–1944)

11

Huldah: prophetess of doom

> Huldah declared to them, 'Thus says the Lord, the God of Israel: Tell the man who sent you to me, Thus says the Lord, I will indeed bring disaster on this place and on its inhabitants – all the words of the book that the king of Judah has read. Because they have abandoned me and have made offerings to other gods, so that they have provoked me to anger with all the work of their hands, therefore my wrath will be kindled against this place, and it will not be quenched.'
>
> 2 KINGS 22:15–17

There are occasions in life when we receive news that we don't want to hear, news that we know will change our lives from that moment on: a diagnosis of a terminal illness, the death of a loved one, a global pandemic. When King Josiah was handed a long-lost manuscript that had been unearthed from the ruins of the temple, he knew that his life, and the life of all his people, was about to be transformed. It was bad news. Huldah was the prophetess who was called upon to impart just how bad this news was to be.

Huldah was a woman from Judah who lived in Jerusalem with her husband Shallum. He was 'keeper of the wardrobe', a job which probably involved looking after the robes of the priests, rather like a verger would in our churches today. They lived during the turbulent times of a seemingly endless cycle of corrupt and cruel kings ruling the divided nations of Israel and Judah. During this period the temple in Jerusalem had been allowed to fall into ruin, the people had turned again to idolatry, and the laws and statutes given to Moses had largely been forgotten.

Josiah was one of the few kings who 'did what was right in the sight of the Lord' (2 Kings 22:2), ruling with justice and equity, ensuring those who worked on the restoration of the temple were paid, and that all the temple funds were accounted for properly. Yet all this was not enough to prevent the catastrophe that was to come.

When the king heard the words from the rediscovered 'book of the law' (the book of Deuteronomy) read to him, he realised with remorse how far his people had turned from God's will. He wanted to understand more and, as Huldah was clearly well known in the community as a prophet, his priests sent for her to help interpret what they were reading. Huldah spoke with authority, clarity and boldness, and did not hide the gravity of what God was saying to them, that Judah would soon be destroyed: 'Because they have abandoned me and have made offerings to other gods, so that they have provoked me to anger with all the work of their hands, therefore my wrath will be kindled against this place, and it will not be quenched.'

The only good news for Josiah was that, because of his repentance, humility and remorse, the inevitable destruction would be delayed until after his death. Huldah's prophetic words came to pass, and soon after Josiah died the kingdom of Judah was decimated by two Babylonian invasions. By the end of the book of Kings, the once-glorious rule of David and Solomon was in ruins. The king (Jehoiachin) was imprisoned; the priests, leaders and craftsmen were exiled; the temple and city walls were destroyed; and even the remaining treasures of Solomon's splendid era were melted down.

There wouldn't be another king in Judah until a very different king came along, also from David's lineage. This king was born into poverty and was led to his death with a crown of thorns on his head, and his resurrection would be the ultimate good news for all people.

Reflection

A friend of mine is an oncologist and often has to pass on the worst possible news, something he never gets used to. Not many people relish the role of 'prophet of doom', and it takes great courage. Huldah joins the other great prophets of the Bible, such as Jonah, Daniel and Micah, who tell the truth even though their message is hard to hear.

When we hear really bad news, often there is not much we can do about the situation itself – a loved one remains sick, a conflict continues, a pandemic rolls on. But we do have a choice as to how we respond to it. Josiah chose to respond to Huldah's words by falling to his knees in prayer and following God 'with all his heart and all his soul' (2 Kings 23:3). Perhaps that is a good place to start.

Prayer

Speak, Lord, for thy servant heareth. Grant us ears to hear, eyes to see, wills to obey, hearts to love; then declare what thou wilt, reveal what thou wilt, command what thou wilt, demand what thou wilt. Amen

Christina Rossetti (1830–94)

Hesed

There is a beautiful word in Hebrew which describes the love that people have towards one another, and also the love God has for humanity. It's not easy to translate into English: it is akin to kindness but is also used to describe loyalty, faithfulness, steadfast devotion, sacrifice and mercy. *Hesed* is one of the core values in the Old Testament, being mentioned there over 200 times, and is rarely used to describe an abstract emotion – it is a deeply practical kind of love, borne out by action. This love is revealed and experienced in many ways through the women of the Old Testament. There is the complicated love of siblings (Rachel, Leah), the faithful love of loyal friendship (Naomi, Ruth), and the sacrificial love that puts another person or God before themselves (Michal, Jephthah's daughter). We also see the painful consequences of a life where love is absent, such as for the unfortunate first Mrs Samson.

⇒ 12 ⇐

Rachel: the sister who was loved

W hile he was still speaking with them, Rachel came with her father's sheep; for she kept them. Now when Jacob saw Rachel, the daughter of his mother's brother Laban, and the sheep of his mother's brother Laban, Jacob went up and rolled the stone from the well's mouth, and watered the flock of his mother's brother Laban. Then Jacob kissed Rachel, and wept aloud. And Jacob told Rachel that he was her father's kinsman, and that he was Rebekah's son; and she ran and told her father.

GENESIS 29:9–12

If anyone thinks the Old Testament is dull, they haven't read the story of Rachel and Leah. It involves mistaken identity, sisterly jealousy, a deceitful father and even unusual aphrodisiac plants! We probably all know the story of Joseph and his many brothers, even if only from the musical. But what do we know of Joseph's mother, and the (three) mothers of the other brothers?

Leah and Rachel were the daughters of Laban, Rebekah's brother. Leah was the eldest, her 'eyes were lovely' (or 'weak', depending on the translation); Rachel 'was graceful and beautiful' (Genesis 29:17). Jacob was on the run from his twin brother Esau and fled to his uncle Laban in the hope of finding a wife. He found two!

There is little doubt that Jacob loved his cousin Rachel with a passion rarely seen in Old Testament relationships, and their initial encounter is gloriously romantic. Rachel was going about her daily chores of looking after her father's sheep when Jacob saw her by the well and, realising she was one of his family, immediately went up to her, kissed her 'and wept aloud'. He then helped her by rolling back the large stone over the well, shared his story with her and received an invitation back to her father's house. A romantic start, perhaps, but their relationship was far from 'happily ever after'.

Jacob had to work on Laban's farm for seven years to earn the right to marry his daughter. Then, when the time was up, and the marriage celebrations were underway, in an action that would change the course of the sisters' lives forever, Laban sent Leah into the tent instead of Rachel. It was dark and Leah would have been heavily veiled, so Jacob didn't realise the deceit until too late. In that culture, this meant that he was now married to her, even though she was the wrong woman.

Laban allowed Jacob to marry Rachel the next week after making him pledge to work for him for another seven years. The sisters had no choice in all of this, of course. Having multiple wives was common in the culture of the time, but it isn't hard to imagine how difficult it must have been for them, and Rachel became bitter and envious.

Jacob loved Rachel more than Leah, but Leah was able to have children more easily. At one stage, Rachel became so despairing that she cried out to her husband, 'Give me children or I shall die!' (Genesis 30:1). She did have children eventually, two surrogate sons through her maid Bilhah and then a child of her own, the beloved Joseph. It appears that Rachel never found peace, though, and was consumed by her yearning for more children and subsequent bitterness towards her sister. Her longed-for second child did arrive, but sadly she didn't survive the birth. Her final act was to name him Ben-oni, which means 'son of my sorrow', a name that revealed so much about this beautiful but deeply sad woman.

Thankfully for the baby, Jacob overruled the name and called him Benjamin, which means 'son of my right hand'. The tribe of Benjamin became one of the most significant tribes for the people of Israel, and it was from here that the first king of Israel, Saul, emerged.

Rachel was buried on the way to Bethlehem, and her tomb is a significant site for pilgrims to this day.

Reflection

Rachel's life wasn't easy. Women in the ancient world were expected to produce offspring, and their prosperity and happiness depended upon this. Let us pray for all those who continue to be defined by their fertility, and for those who seem to never find contentment in life.

Prayer

Oh God, you have called us to be your people. You have loved us and chosen us for your own. Clothe us with your compassion, kindness, humility, gentleness and patience. Help us be tolerant and to forgive one another as you have forgiven us. And bind us all together in the perfect unity of your love. Amen
Adapted from COLOSSIANS 3:12–14 (GNT)

❧ 13 ❧

Leah: the other sister

When the Lord saw that Leah was unloved, he opened her womb; but Rachel was barren. Leah conceived and bore a son, and she named him Reuben; for she said, 'Because the Lord has looked on my affliction; surely now my husband will love me.' She conceived again and bore a son, and said, 'Because the Lord has heard that I am hated, he has given me this son also'; and she named him Simeon. Again she conceived and bore a son, and said, 'Now this time my husband will be joined to me, because I have borne him three sons'; therefore he was named Levi. She conceived again and bore a son, and said, 'This time I will praise the Lord'; therefore she named him Judah; then she ceased bearing.

GENESIS 29:31–35

Much of my childhood was spent arguing with my sister. I am three years older than her and was deeply jealous, to the extent that when she was born I started to sleep outside my parents' bedroom door so that I was first to be seen in the morning! I don't look back on those years with pride, as I was pretty vile to her, and one of the greatest blessings in my life is that we're now the best of friends. But this certainly wouldn't be the case if we were married to the same man!

Leah was the eldest, and yet she was always in second place to her beautiful younger sibling: '[Jacob] loved Rachel more than Leah' (Genesis 29:30). There is ample evidence in the text of Rachel's jealousy towards Leah, but very little the other way around. Unlike her sister, Leah found it easy to conceive and was blessed with six sons and a daughter, and yet after each birth she reveals her deepest desire. Leah's focus wasn't on her sister, but on her husband and on her longing for him to love her.

Her cries are painful: 'Surely now my husband will love me' and 'This time my husband will be joined to me.' Even after her sixth son is born her focus remains on Jacob: 'Now my husband will honour me, because I have borne him six sons' (Genesis 30:20). Sadly, there is nothing to say that Jacob changed his affections, and he even favoured Rachel's sons over Leah's – we remember the consequence of this within the story of Joseph.

Although neither Rachel nor Leah had much say over who they were to marry, it seems that they did have agency within their relationship. They were the ones to name their sons, for example, and they were also able to control which of the two of them Jacob slept with. On one occasion Leah wanted to conceive again and the only way she could do this was to barter with Rachel using some mandrakes, a known ancient aphrodisiac said to possess natural stimulants: 'When Jacob came from the field in the evening, Leah went out to meet him, and said, "You must come in to me; for I have hired you with my son's mandrakes." So he lay with her that night' (Genesis 30:16).

Leah may not have been Jacob's most beloved wife, but she was blessed by God with a quiver full of sons who went on to form the tribes of Israel, and she seems to have been more contented than her sister. Jacob may not have favoured her in life, but in death she was honoured and buried alongside Abraham and Sarah in the place where Jacob would be eventually laid to rest. United in death, if not in life.

Reflection

We don't know if the sisters were ever reconciled, but I like to think that their passionate jealousy and fierce rivalry ran alongside a deep love for one another. They were in an impossible situation and one that would have tested even the closest siblings. Leah's story also reminds us of all those who feel themselves inferior and 'other', particularly within the context of a family. As we reflect on our own sibling and familial relationships, and the complex emotions they stir up within us, we might ask for God's grace, for healing of bitterness and jealousy, and for the ability to forgive.

Prayer

Lord God, in whose glorious kingdom there is no 'second place' and all people are beloved as precious children, bless all those who believe themselves to be inferior, unloved or unwanted, and let them know they are precious in your sight. Amen

14

Naomi: bittersweet

In the days when the judges ruled, there was a famine in the land, and a certain man of Bethlehem in Judah went to live in the country of Moab, he and his wife and two sons. The name of the man was Elimelech and the name of his wife Naomi, and the names of his two sons were Mahlon and Chilion; they were Ephrathites from Bethlehem in Judah. They went into the country of Moab and remained there. But Elimelech, the husband of Naomi, died, and she was left with her two sons. These took Moabite wives; the name of the one was Orpah and the name of the other Ruth. When they had lived there for about ten years, both Mahlon and Chilion also died, so that the woman was left without her two sons or her husband.

RUTH 1:1–5

The Bechdel Test is a measure of the representation of women in fiction and film and asks these three questions: are at least two women featured? Do the women have a conversation with each other? Is that conversation about something or someone other than a man? It's remarkable how many works of literature and film fail this simple test! The book of Ruth passes the Bechdel Test. It is one of only two books of the Bible named after a woman (the other being Esther), and it is a story about the power of a deep, sacrificial relationship between two grieving women, Naomi and Ruth, and of their journey of friendship, faith and healing.

Naomi and her husband Elimelech lived in Bethlehem in Judah with their two sons, Mahlon and Chilion, at a time when Israel was ruled by the judges (probably Gideon). When a famine hit the region, Elimelech moved his family to Moab, a land with a non-Jewish population. He died soon after arriving there and the sons took Moabite wives and settled. Tragedy struck again and both sons died, leaving Naomi devastated. It is akin to the tragic blows experienced by Job, but Naomi's situation was exacerbated because she was a woman without the protection of a male family member, and she was in a foreign land far from her extended family.

It isn't surprising, then, that Naomi decided to return home to Bethlehem, particularly as the famine was now over. Her two widowed daughters-in-law, Ruth and Orpah, both began the 50-mile journey with her, but at some point along the way

Naomi realised that taking these women far away from their own people would be the wrong thing to do. As they were still young, there was still some hope for them and their future. She encouraged them to return to their families, to find new husbands and rebuild their lives. Naomi had no such hope for herself. She believed that God had turned against her, and her pain was so deep-rooted that she even asked for her name to be changed from Naomi ('delight') to Mara ('bitterness').

After a great deal of persuasion, Orpah tearfully turned back to join her family, but Ruth refused to leave Naomi and 'clung to her' (Ruth 1:14). Naomi eventually relented and the two widows went together back to Bethlehem, where they arrived in time for the harvest. Ruth went to work in the fields gleaning, harvesting the wheat reserved for widows, and the pair began the slow work of healing. This took time for Naomi, but the dual balm of steadfast commitment alongside the practical support offered her by her daughter (as she now saw her) began to bring signs of hope that the bitterness was melting. One of these signs was the energetic support Naomi gave Ruth in securing a husband, Boaz, a match that would enable the land lost through Elimelech's death to be restored to the family.

This wasn't all that was restored to Naomi. By the end of the book she had a secure home, a daughter who loved her and a grandchild. She also had the respect and blessing of her community and, above all this, her faith in God.

Reflection

What is so lovely about Naomi and Ruth's relationship is the mutual reciprocity at the heart of it: Naomi relies on Ruth's support and youthful energy in her time of greatest need; Ruth relies on Naomi's wisdom and contacts in a strange land, and they walk together in their grief. There are few relationships in the Hebrew scriptures which we might wish to emulate today – most of them seem to be marred by rivalry, jealousy and power imbalance – but the friendship between Naomi and Ruth is one of them. It is one of the most beautiful descriptions of loyalty and love in the Bible and it reminds us of the gift that our friends are to us, particularly those friends who have walked alongside us in our darkest moments and who refuse to give up on us even if we push them away in our sadness. Friendships like this are a gift. Let us give thanks for them.

Prayer

Loving God, we thank you for the joy and comfort of friendships:
for those who have been there for us through the ups and downs of life;
for those who have walked beside us even when we've not
been great company; for those who have given us advice
and guidance; and for those friends who are no longer with us
and who we long to meet again. Amen

❧ 15 ❧

Ruth: soft heart, hard feet

> Then they wept aloud again. Orpah kissed [Naomi], but Ruth clung to her. So she said, 'See, your sister-in-law has gone back to her people and to her gods; return after your sister-in-law.' But Ruth said, 'Do not press me to leave you or to turn back from following you! Where you go, I will go; where you lodge, I will lodge; your people shall be my people, and your God my God. Where you die, I will die – there will I be buried. May the Lord do thus and so to me, and more as well, if even death parts me from you!'
>
> RUTH 1:14–17

As a young Christian I was transfixed by the story of Jackie Pullinger. In 1966, when she was in her early 20s, she was called by God to leave her home and family in London, and she set off on a boat with a one-way ticket to Hong Kong without any idea of what she would do when she got there. She then lived and worked in the infamous Kowloon Walled City, among drug users and triad gangs, and developed a ministry which continues to this day. She was one of the first female role models I can remember, and what attracted me was her bravery and willingness to go where she believed God was calling her, even though that came with huge risks to her own life. In her book *Chasing the Dragon*, she writes, 'God wants us to have soft hearts and hard feet. The trouble with so many of us is that we have hard hearts and soft feet.'

Ruth had both a soft heart *and* hard feet. She was a non-Jewish woman from Moab, whose Jewish husband had died, leaving her with a bitterly grieving mother-in-law, Naomi, and a sister-in-law, Orpah, whose husband had also died. When her mother-in-law chose to return to her homeland, Ruth made the brave decision to move away from all she knew in order to go with her. In deciding to bind herself to Naomi, she also made a commitment to Naomi's community and to God. Her prayer of conversion is beautiful: 'Where you go, I will go; where you lodge, I will lodge; your people shall be my people, and your God my God. Where you die, I will die - there will I be buried.' What a powerful declaration of loving commitment from one person to another.

Ruth chose to accompany Naomi and was willing to step into the unknown, into a life that was unpredictable and precarious, to go to a foreign land where she would be vulnerable and unprotected. Her motivations for doing this are unclear. Did she stay with Naomi because of her deep love and affection for this older, and in many ways needy, woman? Or did Ruth have a sense of God's call on her life that meant that she knew deep down in her soul that she should leave Moab?

Whatever her reason, Ruth's brave decision led her to Bethlehem where, while in the fields gathering food, she encountered Boaz, a distant relative of Naomi's. Boaz protected her from harm, and Naomi encouraged their blossoming romance and even advised her on how to secure his affection: 'Now wash and anoint yourself, and put on your best clothes and go down to the threshing-floor' (Ruth 3:3). Ruth and Boaz eventually married, her future was secured and they had a child, Obed, who became the grandfather of King David.

Ruth is one of the small number of women, alongside Tamar, Rahab and Bathsheba, to be named in the genealogy of Jesus.

Reflection

Not many people are called by God to leave everything they've ever known in the way Jackie Pullinger or Ruth were, but we may be able to identify a time when we have been asked to take a step of faith. When I first felt God was calling me to be a priest, I knew that this would mean we would have to leave our comfortable home in an Oxfordshire village, a decision that was harder to make because we had three young boys at the time. It's tempting at times to wonder what might have been if we had taken other paths in life, but Jesus' call to his disciples is always to follow, to look forward, to put the hand to the plough and to not look back (Luke 9:62).

Prayer

Gracious God, you have called us to life and gifted us in many ways. Guide us to choose the way of life you have planned for each one of us and give us the courage to go where you lead. May we, with soft hearts and hard feet, be faithful to your call. Amen

16

The first Mrs Samson

On the fourth day they said to Samson's wife, 'Coax your husband to explain the riddle to us, or we will burn you and your father's house with fire. Have you invited us here to impoverish us?' So Samson's wife wept before him, saying, 'You hate me; you do not really love me. You have asked a riddle of my people, but you have not explained it to me.' He said to her, 'Look, I have not told my father or my mother. Why should I tell you?' She wept before him for the seven days that their feast lasted; and because she nagged him, on the seventh day he told her. Then she explained the riddle to her people.

JUDGES 14:15–17

Marriages in ancient societies, like in the Old Testament, were often arranged between families. They were a way of fostering peace or unity between communities, or for prestige and financial reasons. In these societies, marriages could be arranged in consultation with the couple, and lead to a happy, fulfilled relationship. Sadly, this was not the case for Samson's first wife.

We all know tales of weddings gone awry. A vicar friend of mine dropped the ring down the church grate during the vows. They had to use a bridesmaid's ring until they could get in a plumber after the service! However, I don't think anyone will have had a worse engagement and wedding than the poor first Mrs Samson. Most people have never heard of her, and she doesn't aspire to the fame of her successor Delilah. She isn't even named – she is just 'a Philistine woman' (Judges 14:1).

Samson, the nazirite known for his strength, saw her from afar and decided that he wanted her as his wife. It wasn't the most romantic start, as he commanded his parents to 'get her for me' (Judges 14:3). At the time the Philistines and Israelites were enemies, so this was an unusual match and both families were wary. It began badly. On the way to meet her, Samson encountered a lion and ripped it apart with his bare hands. On the way home, he took the honey that he found in the carcass as a gift for his parents. This act went against one of the core nazirite vows which, alongside not cutting their hair, was to have no contact with anything dead.

But things really began going wrong during the wedding reception, which in those times lasted several days. The Philistines provided Samson with 30 young men to be his companions during the festivities, and he decided to set them up with a riddle using fine linens as a wager: 'Out of the eater came something to eat. Out of the strong came something sweet' (Judges 14:14).

This perplexed the young men to the extent they grew wild with frustration. So wild, in fact, that they threatened to murder the bride and burn her family home if she didn't tell them the answer! She cried for the whole seven days of her 'celebrations' and eventually persuaded her new husband to give her the answer (lion, honey), which she passed on to the men. Sadly, this didn't end the matter. Samson was so furious that he'd lost the riddle that he paid back his debt by stealing the clothes off the backs of another group of men, and then angrily stormed back to his family home, abandoning his new bride. She was then given in marriage to one of the companions.

One can imagine she might have been relieved to be rid of the unpredictable nazirite for good. However, the next year Samson went back to reclaim his bride and, finding she was already married, began a cycle of violence between the two clans, which led to arguably the most bizarre act of revenge in the entire Bible. Samson caught 300 foxes (how on earth did he manage this?), tied their tails together, set them alight and let them loose in the Philistines' fields, where they ran around burning down all their crops. The Philistines retaliated by murdering Samson's ill-fated first wife, her father and many of her people.

And it all began with a riddle!

Reflection

The first Mrs Samson reminds us that many women down the centuries, and still today, find themselves in loveless marriages and have little or no control over their lives. Lifelong marriage can be a challenge, and couples need the help and support of those around them. This is why the Church of England's wedding service includes a vow made by all those at the ceremony: 'Will you family and friends of [the couple] support and uphold them now and in the years to come?'

Prayer

Almighty God, giver of life and love, bless all those you have joined in marriage and lifelong partnership. Grant them wisdom and devotion in their life together; may they be to the other a strength in need, a comfort in sorrow, a companion in joy; and may those for whom marriage is a source of pain know your comfort and healing love. Amen

17

Jephthah's daughter: a deadly promise

> Then Jephthah came to his home at Mizpah; and there was his daughter coming out to meet him with timbrels and with dancing. She was his only child; he had no son or daughter except her. When he saw her, he tore his clothes, and said, 'Alas, my daughter! You have brought me very low; you have become the cause of great trouble to me. For I have opened my mouth to the Lord, and I cannot take back my vow.'
>
> JUDGES 11:34–35

There are few stories in the Old Testament that are as maddening as the story of Jephthah and his treatment of his daughter. It is the story of a proud father, an innocent daughter and a misguided vow.

Jephthah's daughter loved to dance, and this is how we first meet her, running to greet her father 'with timbrels and with dancing' as he returns victorious from battle. She was the only child of Jephthah, who was himself an exile from the tribe of Gilead, having been disinherited by his half-brothers for being 'the son of another woman' (Judges 11:2). He'd made a home for himself in Tob and had become a successful leader of 'a gang of scoundrels' (Judges 11:3, NIV).

War had broken out. The Gileadites wanted Jephthah's fighting skills and begged him to return to join them, which he reluctantly agreed to do. However, rather than relying on his skill and on prayer, he made a rash vow to God which would be his undoing: 'If you will give the Ammonites into my hand, then whoever comes out of the doors of my house to meet me, when I return victorious from the Ammonites, shall be the Lord's, to be offered up by me as a burnt-offering' (Judges 11:30–31).

What was he thinking? Perhaps he imagined a goat would come out of the house first, or a servant he had no regard for. But he surely can't have intended for it to be his beloved only child. And so when his daughter came out of the house singing and dancing, he cried out in dismay. Not, as you might think, in concern for her, but for himself! 'Alas, my daughter! You have brought me very low; you have become the cause of great trouble to me. For I have opened my mouth to the Lord, and I cannot take back my vow.'

Her reaction was remarkable. She told him that he should not revoke his vow to the Lord and asked for a final two months of freedom to mourn all that she was about to lose. She spent that time with her female friends in the hills, and then went back to her death, and he 'did with her according to the vow he had made' (Judges 11:39). Jephthah's daughter had no choice over what was to happen to her. However, she did have agency over her actions and showed astonishing courage and strength in the face of a terrible injustice done to her by the very person who should have protected her.

We might recall a similar story from Genesis where Isaac was to be sacrificed by his father Abraham. Isaac was saved because an angel appeared just before the final deed, and a ram was sacrificed in his place. Sadly, there was no angel to save Jephthah's daughter.

Reflection

This story raises more questions than answers. Was this sacrifice something that God ordained, or was it just the foolishness and pride of a father unwilling to back down on a promise? Why was she so willing to accept her fate? Why didn't God intervene in the way he did with Isaac?

My view is that this tale reminds us that many terrible things have been done in the name of religion which are nothing to do with God's will. Human sacrifice was forbidden by law in the Torah, and Jephthah would surely have known this. God doesn't intervene because God allows us to make choices in our lives, and at times these choices are destructive and cause untold misery. We would love God to intervene each time we hear of a father abusing or murdering their children, which happens with desperately sad frequency. But God doesn't work like that.

It's a hard story to reflect on, but the Bible doesn't shy away from the gritty reality of life. It's also important to remember in prayer all those who are harmed at the hands of those they trust.

Prayer

Almighty God, loving Father of all, protect those who suffer at the hands of those who should protect them; bless those who work with survivors of domestic abuse; and help us to remember that we have a heavenly Father who loves us and will do us no harm. Amen

100

✴ 18 ✴

Michal: love and hate

Now Saul's daughter Michal loved David. Saul was told, and the thing pleased him. Saul thought, 'Let me give her to him that she may be a snare for him and that the hand of the Philistines may be against him'… David was well pleased to be the king's son-in-law. Before the time had expired, David rose and went, along with his men, and killed one hundred of the Philistines; and David brought their foreskins, which were given in full number to the king, that he might become the king's son-in-law. Saul gave him his daughter Michal as a wife.

1 SAMUEL 18:20–21a, 26b–27

Hesed is often translated as 'loving kindness'. As we saw in the introduction to this section, it's a word that describes the sacrificial love that exists between people, and it also describes the love God has for humankind. Interestingly, the root of the word can mean both passion *for* and *against* someone. Love and hate are closely entwined, and the most passionate love can turn ugly very quickly. Michal's story involves deep sacrificial love, but it's a love that is never truly shared and that turns into profound bitterness, and ultimately to hatred.

Michal was the youngest daughter of Saul, the first king of Israel, and she is the only woman in the entire Bible to be described as being romantically in love: 'Michal loved David.' At the time David was a handsome young warrior in her father's household, rapidly gaining power, authority and acclaim. Saul's antipathy towards his perceived rival escalated to the stage where everything David did riled him; once, when David was playing his harp, Saul flew into a such a rage that he threw his spear at him!

Saul was delighted with the idea of a union between his daughter and David, as he saw it as an opportunity to get rid of him. In those days it was customary for the groom to offer a marriage gift to the father of the bride, but Saul demanded 'no marriage present except a hundred foreskins of the Philistines' (1 Samuel 18:25). What a gruesome request! There is no doubt that Saul was hoping that David would be killed in the process of collecting this macabre gift, but in fact David hands over double this, and the marriage takes place.

Saul's rages did not cease after Michal's marriage. They became increasingly violent and unpredictable and David was no longer safe in the palace. Michal and her brother Jonathan, David's beloved friend, at great personal risk to themselves, conspired to help him escape, which he did by climbing through a window while Michal placed a mannequin in his bed to give him time to get away.

This act of *hesed* saved David's life, but Michal lost the man she once loved. She was then given in marriage to another man, Paltiel, but once David became king, he demanded she be brought back to him. Paltiel was bereft and followed behind her, weeping, before being sent away.

Any love that Michal had towards David was a distant memory by the end of their relationship. Like her father before her, she too became irritated by David and his behaviour. Once, when David returned triumphant from battle, he was so happy that he 'danced before the Lord with all his might' (2 Samuel 6:14). Michal watched, unimpressed, from a window. David was probably expecting a hero's welcome from his wife, but instead received the full force of her fury: Michal 'despised him in her heart'. She accused him of being vulgar and 'uncovering himself… before the eyes of his servants' maids'. The argument descended as so many marital rows do. He told her he could celebrate before the Lord however he liked. Hurtful words said in the heat of an argument can't easily be taken back again.

Sadly, Michal and David's relationship never recovered, and the last we hear is that 'Michal… had no children to the day of her death' (2 Samuel 6:23).

Reflection

> For the mountains may depart and the hills be removed,
> but my steadfast love shall not depart from you.
> ISAIAH 54:10

In Michal we see a woman who displays a full range of human emotions. She was willing to dedicate her life to David, but by the end even the way he danced drove her mad with annoyance. Her story reminds us of the delicate nature of human love, and of how painful it is when love turns sour. Thankfully God's *hesed* is unwavering and steadfast. It is a love which is poured out for each one of us and fully revealed in the ultimate sacrifice made by Jesus through his death on the cross.

Prayer

Ah, blessed Lord, I wish I know how I might best love you
and please you, and that my love were as sweet to you
as your love is to me.
Margery Kempe (c. 1373–1438)

'Strident' women

After speaking to the United Nations about climate change, the 16-year-old activist Greta Thunberg was accused on social media of being too strident. 'Strident' is one of those gendered terms, like 'bossy' or 'shrill', that is rarely used to describe men but is often applied to powerful or persuasive women in a derogatory way. The Old Testament world was patriarchal, but a few women did hold power and could enact change. There are many examples of powerful women in this section, such as Zelophehad's daughters, who worked together to change land laws, Jael, who struck the final blow in battle, and Abigail, who showed remarkable peace-making skills. Queen Esther used her powerful position to prevent a genocide, and the Queen of Sheba travelled the world in search of wisdom. Let's find out more about the 'strident' women of the Bible.

❧ 19 ☙

The daughters of Zelophehad: girl power

Then the daughters of Zelophehad came forward. Zelophehad was… a member of the Manassite clans. The names of his daughters were: Mahlah, Noah, Hoglah, Milcah, and Tirzah. They stood before Moses, Eleazar the priest, the leaders, and all the congregation, at the entrance of the tent of meeting, and they said, 'Our father died in the wilderness; he was not among the company of those who gathered themselves together against the Lord in the company of Korah, but died for his own sin; and he had no sons. Why should the name of our father be taken away from his clan because he had no son? Give to us a possession among our father's brothers.'

NUMBERS 27:1–4

One of our family treats is going to see musical theatre, and for our son's birthday we went to see *Fiddler on the Roof* at the Playhouse Theatre in London. It was wonderful. The story revolves around the Jewish patriarch Tevye and his five daughters, all of whom need husbands and dowries, which Tevye, despite pleading to God in the classic song 'If I were a rich man', can't afford. This was a rather similar situation for Zelophehad, who 'had no sons, but daughters: and the names of the daughters of Zelophehad were Mahlah, Noah, Hoglah, Milcah, and Tirzah' (Numbers 26:33). These are women you're unlikely to have ever heard of, but their chutzpah transformed the lives of women down the centuries.

The family lived at a time when the Israelites had been led out of Egyptian slavery by Moses. They had been wandering in the wilderness for 'forty years' (which in the Bible generally means 'a long time') and were about to enter the promised land. But in this story, as soon as Zelophehad is introduced, we find that he has died (Numbers 27:3).

It is a classic patriarchal society. Israel was organised into tribes which were descended from the twelve sons of Jacob. Each tribe was then made up of a number of clans bearing the name of the senior male. Moses decided to take a census of all the tribes so that when they came into the land it could be divided fairly. Zelophehad was from the tribe of Manasseh, and as he had died without sons the custom was that the land that would have been due to him would pass on to another clan. But his daughters decided that this wasn't good enough: 'The daughters of Zelophehad came forward.'

In an act of extraordinary bravery, they left the tented area reserved for women and went to the sacred area where the high-ranking male leaders congregated. This action was bold in itself, but they then further defied custom by speaking up and arguing the case for the reform of inheritance laws. Their reasoning was forthright, concise, personal and persuasive. It ended with their plea: 'Why should the name of our father be taken away from his clan because he had no son? Give to us a possession among our father's brothers.'

Moses didn't know how to answer them, and so he prayed about it and heard from the Lord: 'The daughters of Zelophehad are right in what they are saying; you shall indeed let them possess an inheritance' (Numbers 27:7). The daughters were right! The laws were changed and from then on daughters could inherit at the death of their father and, furthermore, they would be allowed to choose their own husbands – 'Let them marry whom they think best' (Numbers 36:6) – as long as they were from within their own clan. The daughters were faithful to this edict and, some years later in the time of Joshua, they were justly apportioned their own land alongside all the other male clan leaders (Joshua 17:4).

Reflection

We must not underestimate the importance of the actions of these brave women in changing the lives of so many others down the generations. Ownership of land is still vitally important in ensuring prosperity, particularly in rural communities. Gender inequality in inheritance law and land ownership rights is still a current issue, and one of the UN's Sustainable Development Goals is to address this.[3] It is unlikely that these five women would have been heard as individuals: their voices had more power together. They remind us of the power of groups to bring about change, of the importance of stepping forward in faith and speaking up against injustice, and of the encouraging fact that sometimes when we do, things change.

Prayer

God of wisdom and boldness,
we give you thanks for those in every age
who have rejected what was expected of them
to fight for their own life and for the future of those in need.
Teach us to discern where our voices are needed
and let us be people of courage and bringers of hope.
Philippa White

⟫⟫ 20 ⟪⟪

Jael: lethal in tent

N ow Sisera had fled away on foot to the tent of Jael wife of Heber the Kenite; for there was peace between King Jabin of Hazor and the clan of Heber the Kenite. Jael came out to meet Sisera, and said to him, 'Turn aside, my lord, turn aside to me; have no fear.' So he turned aside to her into the tent, and she covered him with a rug. Then he said to her, 'Please give me a little water to drink; for I am thirsty.' So she opened a skin of milk and gave him a drink and covered him.

JUDGES 4:17–19

The 2013 *New York Times*' annual of obituaries is intriguingly titled *The Socialite Who Killed a Nazi with Her Bare Hands*.[4] It featured the obituary of Nancy Wake, who joined the French Resistance during World War II. She saved the lives of hundreds of Allied soldiers and airmen by helping them escape through France to Spain, and she once killed an SS sentry to prevent him from raising an alarm. After the war she told an interviewer: 'I don't see why we women should just wave our men a proud goodbye and then knit them balaclavas.' [5]

Jael shatters any illusions we may have that women are incapable of active combat. The book of Judges contains some of the most gruesome accounts of human violence imaginable. It's a challenging read, not least because as Christians we are uncomfortable with the idea that God seems to reward and even command the violence. Jael's story is even more surprising, because here the violent killing of a general as he rested from his exertions is carried out by a woman.

Jael was the wife of a metalworker called Heber. They were Kenites, Israelite by ancestry, but Heber had defected to the Canaanites. Sisera, the commander of Canaan's army, was in retreat. His 900 chariots, thrown into confusion by floods, had been swamped by Barak and Deborah's ten thousand soldiers. His army was in chaos, and he fled on foot to the safety of the camp of his long-time ally.

Heber may well have been an ally, but he wasn't at home and so Sisera was greeted by his wife Jael. It seems that her sympathies were with the people of Israel, who had suffered 20 years of oppression under Canaan's rule.

Jael used her charm to lull Sisera into a false sense of security: 'Turn aside, my Lord, turn aside to me; have no fear.' She was generous and hospitable, gave him some milk and a warm bed, and tucked him in for the night. After a full day's battle, Sisera was exhausted and he soon fell sound asleep. Bedouin people lived in tents, so Jael's weapon of choice would have been close at hand: '[She] went softly to him and drove the peg into his temple, until it went down into the ground… and he died' (Judges 4:21).

Deborah's earlier prophecy that Sisera's defeat would come at the hands of a woman came true, and shortly after his death the rest of the Canaanite army fell. Yahweh had heard the cry of his people and saved them once again, but this time he had used the hands of two women to fulfil his purposes. As a result of their actions 'the land had peace for forty years' (Judges 5:31, NIV).

That is, until the people rebelled against God and war broke out once again (Judges 6).

Reflection

Put on the full armour of God.
EPHESIANS 6:13 (NIV)

One of the most troubling aspects of the Old Testament is the issue of violence. Does the God of love really command genocide? Has God changed over time, or has our understanding of the nature of God changed? These are difficult questions to answer, but delving into the most dark and violent stories like this one reminds us of the enduring character of God. God does not tolerate evil and hates it when people worship other gods and oppress the people he loves. Alongside this, God will always have compassion when people cry out to him. In parts of the Old Testament such as this, God's purposes are carried out by means of warfare, but as Christians we are given a different type of armour to fight with. Our world is still violent and evil, but our weapons aren't chariots or tent pegs; they are truth, righteousness, peace, faith, salvation, scripture and prayer (Ephesians 6:10–18).

Prayer

God of Jael, in the chaos of a violent world
your still small voice promises a new creation,
where all may serve you in freedom and without fear.
Make us people of truth and peace
to tell the good news of your coming kingdom
and make known your liberating love.
Philippa White

21

Abigail: the desert diplomat

When Abigail saw David, she hurried and alighted from the donkey, and fell before David on her face, bowing to the ground. She fell at his feet and said, 'Upon me alone, my lord, be the guilt; please let your servant speak in your ears, and hear the words of your servant. My lord, do not take seriously this ill-natured fellow, Nabal; for as his name is, so is he; Nabal is his name, and folly is with him; but I, your servant, did not see the young men of my lord, whom you sent… And now let this present that your servant has brought to my lord be given to the young men who follow my lord. Please forgive the trespass of your servant.'

1 SAMUEL 25: 23–25, 27–28a

Christine de Pizan (1364–1430) wrote that 'women particularly should concern themselves with peace because men by nature are more foolhardy and head-strong, and their overwhelming desire to avenge themselves prevents them from foreseeing the resulting dangers and terrors of war'.[6] Women down the centuries have mediated between feuding men, and Abigail is a wonderful example of this.

At a time when the Israelites were desert tribes, Saul was king and David was a fugitive gaining power, Nabal, the villain of the tale, was a wealthy sheep farmer. David and his men protected the area against predators and thieves. Nabal was married to Abigail, a woman gifted with wisdom and tact, described as 'clever and beautiful' (1 Samuel 25:3). Nabal, on the other hand, was rich, charmless and boorish. His name literally means 'fool' or 'moron', and he certainly lived up to it.

It was sheep-shearing season, traditionally a time when communities would hold celebration feasts. David sent ten men to ask for some produce for the feast as a neighbourly reward for having protected Nabal's property, as was customary in those days. Nabal responded to David's request by shouting insults at the men and pretending he didn't know who their master was. David was furious and began making preparations for battle. One of Nabal's men, fearing the ensuing danger and realising that there was no point talking to Nabal, who was 'so ill-natured that no one can speak to him' (1 Samuel 25:17), went directly to Abigail.

Abigail gathered a number of gifts, loaded up the donkeys and went to meet David and his men. She threw herself at David's feet and then, in one of the longest recorded speeches by a woman in the Old Testament, delivered a brilliant and eloquent peace-making argument. Her reasoning appealed to David's pride and was both theologically compelling and strategically sensible. She was respectful and deferential; she was humble and asked for forgiveness; she offered gifts; and finally she reminded David that his life's purpose was to serve God, that one day he would be 'prince over Israel' and so should remain pure (1 Samuel 25:31).

Abigail's speech changed David's mind, and he turned back with the words: 'Blessed be your good sense… I have heeded your voice' (1 Samuel 25:33, 35).

What Abigail did that day was hugely risky and brave; her meeting with David could have backfired with terrible consequences. Alongside this, she also risked the wrath of her husband. Once she returned home, she told him what she had done. He was so shocked 'his heart died within him; he became like a stone' (1 Samuel 25:37). It is likely that he had a stroke or a heart attack, and ten days later he died.

Abigail's shrewd actions prevented many lives from being lost, but the story doesn't end there. David, hearing of Nabal's demise, sent for her and she became his third wife and the mother of his second son.[7]

Reflection

As we remember Abigail, let us pray for all those who are peacemakers, for those who do this on a global and national stage, and for those involved in conflict mediation on a local level. Let us also remember those who are today living with partners whose behaviour is unpredictable and violent, and who struggle to maintain peace in their own homes.

Prayer

O God, from whom all holy desires,
all good counsels, and all just works do proceed;
Give unto thy servants that peace
which the world cannot give;
that our hearts may be set to obey thy commandments,
and also that by thee, we,
being defended from the fear of our enemies,
may pass our time in rest and quietness;
through the merits of Jesus Christ our Saviour. Amen
The Collect for Peace from The Book of Common Prayer

22

The queen of Sheba: wisdom seeker

When the queen of Sheba heard of the fame of Solomon, (fame due to the name of the Lord), she came to test him with hard questions. She came to Jerusalem with a very great retinue, with camels bearing spices, and very much gold, and precious stones; and when she came to Solomon, she told him all that was on her mind. Solomon answered all her questions; there was nothing hidden from the king that he could not explain to her.

1 KINGS 10:1–3

The queen of Sheba is well-known, but the detail in the Bible is actually rather scant and most of what we know about her is taken from legend, poetry, art and myth. In Ethiopian tradition she is called Makeda, and in Islamic and Yemeni tradition she is Bilquis. She is undoubtedly the most exotic and enigmatic woman of this book, and markedly different to all the other women: a female ruler from a far-flung land, fabulously wealthy and, apparently, independent of any man or particular social group. Alongside this, what sets her apart is that her journey is one of intellectual curiosity over and above anything else. She is a woman who loved wisdom and was willing to travel the world to seek it out.

The kingdom of Sheba (or Saba) was, together with Tyre and Israel, one of the trading powers of the day. Scholars believe it was situated to the south of the Arabian desert in modern-day Yemen, although some claim she was from Ethiopia. Whichever is true, it is evident it was well placed to trade in gold, silver and spices between Asia, Africa and countries to the north. The queen had heard reports, probably from travelling tradesmen, that King Solomon was the wisest man in the east. She wanted to meet him for herself and so set off on the long journey to Jerusalem.

She arrived at Solomon's temple with a huge entourage, which included camels, spices, precious stones and gold. These were gifts for the king and would have been expected of a royal visit. Her main interest in the king doesn't seem to have been his wealth or huge palace, but rather pure intellectual curiosity: 'She told him all that was on her mind. Solomon answered all her questions; there was nothing hidden.'

She was impressed by Solomon's intellect and wisdom, and by the way he managed his empire. This led her to turn to praise God for all that she saw: 'Blessed be the Lord your God, who has delighted in you and set you on the throne of Israel!' (1 Kings 10:9).

The gifts of gold, spices and precious stones were handed over and then the queen, having learned all that she could from Solomon, set off back to her homeland.

Reflection

One of the many reasons I love my job as a university chaplain is being in the midst of so many young people who are thirsty for knowledge and who are dedicating their lives to learning and seeking understanding. Like the queen of Sheba, they travel from around the globe in the hope of finding some of their questions answered.

There is a difference between knowledge and wisdom, though. Knowledge can be gained through reading, research and gathering information, but wisdom uses discernment, judgement and understanding to take this information and to use it for good. I often marvel at how the cleverest of people can make the most foolish decisions at times!

One of the great things about getting older is knowing that wisdom often comes with maturity, especially if we are willing to learn from our mistakes and to change.

In the book of Proverbs wisdom is personified as a woman who cries out on the streets, calling men and women to the knowledge of God (Proverbs 1:20). Let us pray for wisdom, for ourselves and for our leaders.

Prayer

Almighty God, give us wisdom to perceive you, intellect to understand you, diligence to seek you, patience to wait for you, eyes to behold you, a heart to meditate upon you and life to proclaim you, through the power of the Spirit of our Lord Jesus Christ. Amen

Benedict of Nursia (c. 480–543)

23

Esther: for such a time as this

Mordecai also gave [Hathach] a copy of the written decree issued in Susa for [the Jews'] destruction, that he might…charge her to go to the king to… entreat him for her people.

Hathach went and told Esther what Mordecai had said. Then Esther spoke… 'If any man or woman goes to the king inside the inner court without being called, there is but one law – all alike are to be put to death…' Mordecai told them to reply to Esther, 'Do not think that in the king's palace you will escape any more than all the other Jews. For if you keep silence at such a time as this, relief and deliverance will rise for the Jews from another quarter, but you and your father's family will perish. Who knows? Perhaps you have come to royal dignity for just such a time as this.'

ESTHER 4:8–14

A few years ago I visited Auschwitz-Birkenau in Poland. I will never forget the heaviness of the place, the weight of evil that bears down. The goal of the Nazis was the extermination of the Jewish people. This is not new, and the book of Esther recounts the first attempt at the extermination of Jewish people in 480–460BC.

Later we'll read of Queen Vashti's departure from the Persian King Ahasuerus' palace. This opened the way for one of the greatest heroines of the Hebrew scriptures, Esther, whose story is retold each year during the festival of Purim.

As a Jewish orphan girl who had been brought up by her uncle Mordecai, Esther was very different from the aristocratic Vashti. The king had sent out his servants to find a replacement wife, and beautiful young women from around the land were taken to the palace to join the harem. These women were prepared for their 'audience' with the king: in reality an abusive system whereby a different girl was taken each night to have sex with the king. His power was absolute, and no one could enter his courts without being called by him, or they risked being put to death.

Esther was 'fair and beautiful', and the king made her queen to replace Vashti. She had a secret, however: she didn't tell anyone that she was Jewish, and she continued to keep in touch with Mordecai, who spent his time sitting at the king's gate, perhaps so that he could hear news of his adoptive daughter.

If this was a fairy tale and Queen Esther was the princess, then the evil villain now comes on the scene: Haman, who was promoted by the king to be his 'first official'. A vain and arrogant man, Haman demanded everyone worship him. When Mordecai, whose loyalty was to God, refused to bow, Haman was furious and used this as an excuse to plot to 'destroy all the Jews, the people of Mordecai' (Esther 3:6). The king passively agreed to his proposal and edicts to kill the Jewish people were sent out. Esther was deeply distressed, and Mordecai asked her to intercede with the king, telling her that she had been put into the palace at 'such a time as this' to help her people. Esther realised that she would have to tread very carefully – she remembered what had happened to Vashti.

Esther took control of the situation, first asking all Jews to fast (and, we assume, pray) for three days. She then went to the king to ask to host a banquet for him and Haman. The king was delighted, offering her anything she desired. Esther disclosed her background and told the king of the ensuing massacre: 'Let my life be given me… and the lives of my people – that is my request' (Esther 7:3–4).

The king's eyes were opened to what was being done is his name, the wicked Haman was killed on his own gallows and the Jewish people were saved. In a final twist to the tale, Mordecai was given Haman's position in the palace and Esther and her uncle were given his house and household: 'There was gladness and joy among the Jews, a festival and a holiday' (Esther 8:17). The festival of Purim was instituted, and every year Esther continues to be remembered.

Reflection

We all face times when we have a choice as to whether to speak up against injustice or to remain silent. I can recall with shame many times when I've chosen the latter path. We are becoming increasingly aware of the continued discrimination faced by other minority groups in our society, such as LGBTQ+ people and black people, and sadly our church communities are still not safe spaces for too many. Esther was perfectly placed to prevent a terrible injustice from happening, but it took courage. Is there a situation where we are being called to speak up? Perhaps we have been put in that place 'for just such a time as this'.

Prayer

O Lord; make yourself known in this time of our affliction, and give me courage, O King of the gods and Master of all dominion! Put eloquent speech in my mouth before the lion… Save us by your hand, and help me, who am alone and have no helper but you, O Lord.
GREEK ESTHER 4:12–14

Bad girls?

There are some Old Testament women who have a reputation for being bad. Sometimes this is clearly evidenced by their actions (Delilah, Athaliah), but there are others whose wholesale condemnation is perhaps a little unfair (Lot's wife, Potiphar's wife, Jezebel). In a society where women were so often expected to be submissive and meek, these women took a different path. God can even use the 'bad girls' of the Bible to bring about his purposes.

24

Lot's wife: the woman who turned

Then the Lord rained on Sodom and Gomorrah sulphur and fire from the Lord out of heaven; and he overthrew those cities, and all the Plain, and all the inhabitants of the cities, and what grew on the ground. But Lot's wife, behind him, looked back, and she became a pillar of salt.

GENESIS 19:24–26

Like many of the women of the Bible, we don't know the name of our next woman, only that she was Lot's wife. We know that she had two daughters and that she lived in Sodom, a town with a distinctly bad reputation. Although we know little about her life, she's mainly remembered for the manner of her death. It's a curious story.

Lot was Abraham's nephew, and he settled in the Plain of Jordan, better known as Sodom, while Abraham settled in the land of Canaan. The angelic visitors who had visited Abraham and Sarah then headed towards the city of Sodom. Lot greeted them and invited them to his home, and his wife provided a feast for them. However, soon the 'men of the city' surrounded the house demanding the visitors be given over to them 'so that we may know them' (Genesis 19:5). Lot refused to allow the men into his home and instead offered them his own virgin daughters.

Much has been written of these passages in relation to sexuality, and they have been used as justification of God's displeasure at same-sex relationships. But this is not a passage about relationships, same-sex or otherwise; it is about violence. The men of Sodom wanted to rape Lot's visitors, so he protected them by horrifyingly offering his own daughters instead. The angelic visitors struck the rampaging Sodomites with blindness so that they couldn't find the door and then urged the family to 'flee for your life; do not look back or stop anywhere in the Plain; flee to the hills, or else you will be consumed' (Genesis 19:17).

As the family duly fled, the cities of Sodom and neighbouring Gomorrah were both destroyed in a shower of 'sulphur and fire', but Lot's wife, who had been running behind them, looked back. She was immediately turned into a pillar of salt.

Why did she look back? Why salt? Perhaps she lacked faith – but this seems overly harsh; the Bible is full of people who lacked faith but who weren't similarly transformed. I wonder if she looked back because she was grieving the place which held all her memories; or maybe she had felt closer to the people in Sodom than to her husband, who would offer up his own daughters in order to protect some visitors; or perhaps she was simply terrified, frozen to the spot by the horror she was seeing.

Reflection

The UN Refugee Agency estimates that there are nearly 80 million people forcibly displaced in the world today, with 37,000 people each day fleeing their countries due to conflict or persecution. Lot's wife reminds us of the thousands of women forced to flee their homes each day due to violence, war or natural disaster. She reminds us of all those who look back and remember those they've left behind.

Prayer

Heavenly Father, you turn your face towards those in trouble and welcome those who turn to you with open arms. Bless all those who face an uncertain future, particularly refugees. Give them your strength and help all your children turn in faith towards your love. Amen

25

Potiphar's wife: the seductress

Now Joseph was handsome and good-looking. And after a time his master's wife cast her eyes on Joseph and said, 'Lie with me.' But he refused and said to his master's wife, 'Look, with me here, my master has no concern about anything in the house, and he has put everything that he has in my hand. He is not greater in this house than I am, nor has he kept back anything from me except yourself, because you are his wife. How then could I do this great wickedness, and sin against God?' And although she spoke to Joseph day after day, he would not consent to lie beside her or to be with her.

GENESIS 39:6b–10

One of the things you quickly notice when reading about the women in the Old Testament is that they are often only allowed one characteristic – jealous sister, childless woman, whore – while the men are much more likely to be complex and multifaceted. Joseph is a good example of this. He was the favoured son of Jacob and Rachel and had been given a special robe so everyone could know his father 'loved [him] more than any of his other children' (Genesis 37:3). Alongside this he was a dreamer, an infuriating sibling to his brothers and probably rather vain. But he was also clever, faithful and resourceful. His character is given flesh and bones, enough to ensure that many centuries later there would even be a musical written about him.

Potiphar's wife, on the other hand, is only one thing: a seductress. We don't get to find out much about her life – whether she had children, whether she was a kind or demanding mistress, or what Potiphar, an officer of the king of Egypt (Pharaoh), was like as a husband. We don't even know her name. It is likely that she lived in luxury as she had servants and a large household, and probably had a lot of time on her hands with not very much to fill it. That is, until a young Hebrew man joined the household and worked his way up the ranks to become the overseer, like a young version of Mr Carson from *Downton Abbey*.

Joseph was obviously attractive, and Mrs Potiphar began to follow him around. One day she propositioned him directly: 'Lie with me.' The story is told as if this attraction was entirely one-way, but this may well have not been the case. It has all the hallmarks of a *Downton Abbey* upstairs-downstairs affair. However, Joseph knew that if he slept with her he risked his job, his place in the household and even his life: adultery was punishable by death. Joseph was also faithful to God: 'How then could I do this great wickedness, and sin against God?'

Joseph resisted, but Mrs Potiphar persisted, until she turned against him after one rejection too many, and in her anger accused him of attacking her.

We hear nothing more of Potiphar's wife; her role as 'seductress' has been fulfilled. Joseph was summarily thrown into prison, where he began to interpret dreams. This led to him being introduced to Pharaoh himself and becoming the Egyptian king's right-hand man, saving the people from starvation during a season of drought. Mrs Potiphar would surely have encountered Joseph in this role, but we can only guess whether she avoided him or continued to try to seduce the handsome young Hebrew man.

Reflection

Many of the women in the Hebrew scriptures are portrayed as innocent, often silent, victims, but Potiphar's wife breaks the mould. It is easy to be judgemental about such a woman, but it is perhaps helpful to remember that there are numerous stories of men doing far worse than this and to examine whether our sense of moral outrage is proportionate. If it is not, perhaps this is because we still think of women as the 'fairer sex' and find the idea of sexually assertive women uncomfortable.

Prayer

O God our Father, hear me, who am trembling in this darkness, and stretch forth thy hand unto me; hold forth thy light before me; recall me from my wanderings; and thou be my guide, may I be restored to myself and to thee.
Augustine of Hippo (354–430)

26

Delilah: why, why, why?

> After this [Samson] fell in love with a woman in the valley of Sorek, whose name was Delilah. The lords of the Philistines came to her and said to her, 'Coax him, and find out what makes his strength so great, and how we may overpower him, so that we may bind him in order to subdue him; and we will each give you eleven hundred pieces of silver.' So Delilah said to Samson, 'Please tell me what makes your strength so great, and how you could be bound.'
>
> JUDGES 16:4–6a

I'm sure we've all sung along to the Tom Jones classic 'Delilah'. It's a fantastically dark song about a woman caught in adultery and murdered by her lover. The story of Delilah in the book of Judges is also a dark tale, but this time it is the man rather than the woman who ends up dead.

Delilah is a classic example of another female archetype: the femme fatale, a woman who is seductive, intelligent and beautiful. She normally eschews family life, is considered dangerous and uses her wiles to bring about the downfall of a man previously thought to be invincible. We might think of Salome ('give me the head of John the Baptist'), Cleopatra or Carmen. More recent examples are Christine Keeler of the Profumo scandal and Villanelle in *Killing Eve*.

Samson was a judge in Israel at a time when the Israelites were under the domin-ion of the Philistines. His mother had received a prophecy about him at his birth and had dedicated him to God as a nazirite, which meant he would abstain from alcohol, let his hair grow and must not come into contact with the dead. Samson was waging a private battle against the Philistines which culminated in a massive Israelite victory, and he was viewed as the strongest and most powerful hero of his time. He seemed to be invincible. That is, until he met his femme fatale.

Delilah is the only woman in Samson's story who is given a name (ironically it means 'delicate'), and he fell madly in love with her. It is unlikely they were married. The Philistine rulers saw that she could be very useful to them and each offered her an enormous amount of money, 1,100 pieces of silver, in return for information about Samson's weakness so that they could beat him in battle. It's the riddle that he doesn't want anyone to find out: the secret to his strength.

We don't know if Delilah agreed to betray Samson out of loyalty to her people, out of hatred of Samson or for the money. Whatever her motives, she used all of her arts of persuasion to find out his secret: she pleaded – 'Please tell me what makes your strength so great'; she pretended to be hurt – 'You have mocked me and told me lies'; she was assertive – 'Tell me how you could be bound' (Judges 16:13).

Samson played along for a while, giving her three different ways to bind him, using bowstrings, new ropes or locks of hair (Judges 16:7–14). But each time he broke free. She persisted, which, when applied to women, is often called nagging: '"How can you say, 'I love you' when your heart is not with me?"… Finally, after she had nagged him with her words day after day, and pestered him, he was tired to death. So he told her' (Judges 16:15–17).

Once she had the secret, she passed this on to the Philistines, who paid her. She soothed him to sleep on her lap and another man came in and cut his hair off: his strength left him. He was then blinded, thrown into prison and humiliated by being forced to 'entertain' his guards (we don't know exactly what that means). But Samson's hair grew back and his strength returned and, in a final act of power, he pulled the pillars down on them all, killing both himself and his Philistine captors. We don't know if Delilah was among them. I think it's unlikely she stuck around once she'd got her cash. She was far too wily for that!

Reflection

Samson and Delilah had very different ways of showing strength. Samson's strength was physical, yet at times he used this violently and his behaviour towards women revealed some moral shortcomings. Delilah was the physically weaker of the two, but she demonstrated great cunning and powers of persuasion. So it can be with us and others. Some of us look strong on the outside and yet inside are weak and vulnerable; and others are perceived to be weak and yet in adversity turn out to have nerves of steel and an ability to withstand all kinds of trials. The apostle Paul, another powerful man of the Bible, wrote of a physical weakness, 'a thorn in the flesh', with which he struggled and which he asked God to remove from him. This wasn't to be, and he heard God say to him, 'My grace is sufficient for you, for power is made perfect in weakness' (2 Corinthians 12:9).

Prayer

Lord, source of all power, we confess we do not always use the power you give us as you intend; at times we use it to harm others or for our own selfish ends; at other times we are afraid of the power we have and so do not use it at all. Give us the power to be gentle, the strength to be forgiving and the faith to trust that your power is all we need. Amen

27

Jezebel: unfairly judged?

> Ahab told Jezebel all that Elijah had done, and how he had killed all the prophets with the sword. Then Jezebel sent a messenger to Elijah, saying, 'So may the gods do to me, and more also, if I do not make your life like the life of one of them by this time tomorrow.' Then he was afraid; he got up and fled for his life.
>
> 1 KINGS 19:1–3a

The end of Jezebel's life was a tragic one: she was pushed out of her window by Jehu's soldiers and fell to her death, then her body was trampled by horses and eaten by dogs and only her skull, feet and the palms of her hands remained. This was said to have been God's plan as revealed to the prophet Elijah: 'The dogs shall eat Jezebel within the bounds of Jezreel' (1 Kings 21:23).

Jezebel is the only woman of this series with her own dictionary definition. A 'Jezebel' is defined as 'an impudent, shameless or morally unrestrained woman', and her name has long been associated with deceit, sexual immorality, vanity and idol worship. When looking at Jezebel's life, not all of this seems a fair description.

Her story is told in pieces in the Bible, as is usually the way, through the men in her life. She was the daughter of a Phoenician king, Ithobaal, but she moved to Israel on her marriage to King Ahab. It was, as ever, a political marriage. In the Old Testament the sin that most angered the Lord was idolatry, when God's people turned away to worship false gods. Jezebel's people worshipped the nature god Baal-Melkart and she introduced her beliefs and customs to her husband, who took them on with enthusiasm. Many of the Israelite prophets were killed at her command, and those who survived the purges were hidden in a cave and kept alive by a brave Israelite named Obadiah (1 Kings 18).

One of the prophets, Elijah, orchestrated the killing of the priests of Baal, which infuriated Jezebel. She threatened him, declaring, 'May the gods do to me, and more also, if I do not make your life like the life of one of them [i.e. dead] by this time tomorrow.' Elijah was so afraid that he fled into the wilderness, where he hid in a cave until the Lord appeared to him in a 'still small voice' (1 Kings 19:12, KJV) and instructed him to return and anoint Jehu as the next king of Israel.

Jezebel was certainly a force to be reckoned with. One story that reveals this was her ruthless intervention in a neighbourhood dispute. Ahab wanted to buy a vineyard from his neighbour Naboth, as it was in the perfect spot 'for a vegetable garden' (1 Kings 21:2). He offered a good price for it, but Naboth didn't want to sell his ancestral home. Ahab, used to getting his own way, sulked: 'He lay down on his bed, turned away his face, and would not eat' (1 Kings 21:4). Jezebel took decisive action. She forged letters in her husband's name and set a trap for Naboth: he was accused of blasphemy by 'two scoundrels' (1 Kings 21:13). After a show trial which found him guilty, he was taken out and stoned to death. Her plan was stunningly clever because the king could legitimately take the family land of a person accused of blasphemy. It was this murderous act, alongside her idolatry, that led to Elijah's prophecy that God's judgement would come to the pair.

Just before her death, Jezebel appeared at the window, looking down on Jehu, the new king of Israel. When Jezebel heard that Jehu and his army were coming, she didn't run and hide but got ready to face them. She 'painted her eyes, and adorned her head' (2 Kings 9:30), which some interpret to mean that she was attempting to seduce Jehu. The alternative is that she put on her make-up and royal garments in one final show of authority, a last-ditch attempt to maintain some dignity and pride before she fell to her grizzly end. After her death, Jehu killed Ahab's sons and 'wiped out Baal from Israel' (2 Kings 10:28).

Reflection

Jezebel was certainly a fearsome woman. Her choices caused death and misery, but then so did many of those of the men in her story. Yet it is her name that is used to describe immorality and deceit for an entire gender. Is that fair? In fact, there is nothing to suggest she was sexually immoral or unfaithful to her husband: she provided Ahab with children, cared for him and calmed him down when he got angry (1 Kings 21:5). Powerful women often strike fear into men's hearts, and it's a sad reality that, in a male-dominated world, women are all too often relegated to a two-dimensional caricature. Jezebel's legacy is a good example of this. I wonder if she would recognise herself in the role in which she has been cast.

Prayer

Gracious God, though we have not loved you with our whole heart,
nor our neighbours as ourselves,
yet we pray that you would forgive what we have been,
help us to amend what we are,
and direct what we shall be;
through Jesus Christ our Lord. Amen
John Hunter (1849–1917)

❧ **28** ❧

Athaliah: the vengeful queen

> N ow when Athaliah, Ahaziah's mother, saw that her son was dead, she set about to destroy all the royal family. But Jehosheba, King Joram's daughter, Ahaziah's sister, took Joash son of Ahaziah, and stole him away from among the king's children who were about to be killed; she put him and his nurse in a bedroom. Thus she hid him from Athaliah, so that he was not killed; he remained with her for six years, hidden in the house of the Lord, while Athaliah reigned over the land.
>
> 2 KINGS 11:1–3

I once tried reading *Anna Karenina* by Dostoevsky, but I gave up after getting utterly confused by the similarity of so many of the names. Our next woman, Queen Athaliah, appears in a similarly confounding section of the Bible where the characters have names that sound the same, and most seemed to begin with the letters J or A. We have Joram, Jehoram, Jehoshaphat, Jehosheba, Jehoash and Jehoida, and they live in Jezreel. It is further confused by the fact that it is a time when the land is split into the kingdoms of Judah and Israel, and at one stage the kings of both nations had the same name (Jehoram, but sometimes called Joram, in the same passage)!

Athaliah was the daughter of King Ahab and Queen Jezebel of Israel. She was married to King Jehoram of Judah, and it is likely that the marriage was intended to unite the two rival kingdoms. It didn't work out that way. Her husband was a brutal man who had killed his six brothers in order to obtain the throne and her brother was the other Jehoram, the king of Israel at the time.

Athaliah and Jehoram had children, but tragedy struck when a rival faction of rebels seeking independence raided their palace and captured her entire family, leaving only her youngest son, Ahaziah, who eventually succeeded his father to the throne. Ahaziah's rule only lasted a year, as he was assassinated during a state visit to Israel by Jehu (the king of Israel), who ordered the assassination of not only Athaliah's son but also her entire extended family. In a gruesome additional detail, we are told that the heads of the 70 murdered royal princes were placed in a basket and sent as a grisly package to Jehu.

On hearing what had happened to her family, Athaliah doesn't seem to grieve their demise; she was more concerned for power. She proclaimed herself queen of Judah and executed all those who had any royal claim, even killing the women and children. It was a truly horrific period of Israel's history.

Her stepdaughter Jehosheba managed to rescue one of Athaliah's baby grand-children (Joash) from her purge, and he was brought up in secret by a priest named Jehoiada. The priest instigated a rebellion and proclaimed the child king when he was only seven years old. Athaliah was furious and tore her robes, calling out, 'Treason! Treason!' (2 Kings 11:14), but her cries were useless. She was taken out and summarily executed at the gates of the palace: 'and the city was quiet after Athaliah had been killed' (2 Kings 11:20).

Reflection

Athaliah is the only women in this book about whom I've struggled to find a single thing that is commendable or likeable. She was brutal and power hungry and attempted to wipe out the entire line of Judah. Her stepdaughter even had to hide one of her own grandchildren from her for fear that he would be killed. We should note that Athaliah was born into a violent world where both parents were brutally killed and her husband was similarly violent. This might give us some context for her actions, but it is important to remember that women can be thoroughly evil and that terrible crimes have been committed by women, not just against them.

Perhaps all we can do when faced with such evil is to look to the cross, where Jesus took all the pain, violence and suffering of the world on to himself and, surrounded by criminals, cried out, 'Father, forgive them; for they do not know what they are doing' (Luke 23:34).

We can pray for forgiveness. We can remember that Jesus died for the criminal and cruel as well as for those who nurture and care. And we can recognise that each one of us has the capacity to be cruel and violent as well, even if we aren't quite as evil as Athaliah!

Prayer

Oh God the Father of pity, slow to anger with children so swift to sin: deal not with us according to our deserts; but open the arms of your compassion, that what we have lost by our offences we may recover by your mercies, and walk henceforth in your way; through Jesus Christ our Lord.

Daily Prayer, 1941

#ThemToo

It is a sad truth that one of the obvious themes that runs through any book focusing on the lives of women in a patriarchal society is the experience of sexual abuse, harassment and rape. Many of the women featured in this book faced gender-based violence and oppression. Their voices were often not heard (Dinah, Bathsheba) or believed (Susanna), and speaking up came with a cost (Vashti). Sadly this is still the experience of too many women today, as the recent #MeToo and the UK's 'Everyone's Invited' movements have revealed. The stories of the next group of women are difficult ones to read, but they are also a vitally important reminder that we need to continue to listen to the voices of women and survivors of abuse.

29

Dinah: honour or disgrace?

N ow Jacob heard that Shechem had defiled his daughter Dinah; but his sons were with his cattle in the field, so Jacob held his peace until they came. And Hamor the father of Shechem went out to Jacob to speak with him, just as the sons of Jacob came in from the field. When they heard of it, the men were indignant and very angry, because he had committed an outrage in Israel by lying with Jacob's daughter, for such a thing ought not to be done.

GENESIS 34:5–7

'You don't know me, but you've been inside me, and that's why we're here today.' These words form part of a powerful victim impact statement read out in court by 'Emily', a young woman who a year earlier had been sexually assaulted and left, unconscious and naked, behind a bin. Her attacker, a high-flying swimming team hopeful, was given a six-month jail sentence with much made of his glittering career prospects, his good family and the fact they had been drunk. In her statement, 'Emily' recounted the negative effects the assault had on her life: 'You took away my worth, my privacy, my energy, my time, my safety, my intimacy, my confidence, my own voice, until today.'[8]

The account of Dinah involves a rape. It's a troubling story for many reasons, not least due to the nature of the crime, but also because it's hard to know what really happened, as Dinah, unlike Emily, is never given a voice: her story is told entirely through the perspective of the men around her.

Dinah had many men in her life. She was the only daughter of Jacob, born to his first wife Leah, and had six brothers and six half-brothers. The family lived near the city of Shechem in Canaan, and the fledgling community of Israel was learning what it was to be set apart by their faith in Yahweh. The outward sign of this was that all men were circumcised; but they were also considering the rules regarding intermarriage with other tribes in the area. Dinah, perhaps yearning for female company, went out to 'visit the women of the region' (Genesis 34:1).

While in the town she encountered a Hivite prince, also called Shechem. He 'saw her, he took her and raped her' (Genesis 34:3, NIV). The text clearly indicates that the act was violent and against her will, which is why what happens next is so confusing: '[Shechem's] soul was drawn to Dinah daughter of Jacob; he loved the girl, and spoke tenderly to her. So Shechem spoke to his father Hamor, saying, "Get me this girl to be my wife"' (Genesis 34:4).

While Hamor and Jacob were discussing the arrangement, Dinah's brothers came back from work and, finding their sister had been 'defiled', they flew into a shocked and furious rage and refused to allow the marriage to go ahead. Their reasoning was partly because of the 'outrageous thing' that had been done, but also because Shechem had not been circumcised and therefore was an outsider.

The brothers hatched a plan. They told Shechem that the marriage, and other marriages between the Israelites and the locals, could go ahead only if *all* the men in their community were circumcised. Shechem agreed to this and he and the men in the region were circumcised: 'The young man did not delay to do the thing, because he was delighted with Jacob's daughter' (Genesis 34:19).

Two of Dinah's brothers, Simeon and Levi, took full advantage of this, and while the Canaanite men were weak and in pain, they attacked them, killing every male, plundered their homes and seized their women and children. Shechem and Hamor were murdered, and Dinah was 'rescued'. It was another horrific crime.

Reflection

This is a difficult passage to reflect on, but sometimes we need to focus prayerfully on the darkness in our world and remember women who are victims of sexual abuse and rape, and who still struggle to make their voices heard. There is an excellent novel by Anita Diamant called *The Red Tent* (Macmillan, 2001), where Dinah's story is imagined differently, with Dinah and Shechem in love with each other. Her brothers are blinded by rage, pride and the assumption their beloved sister couldn't possibly have willingly had sex with an outsider. Diamant's version is clearly an imagined story, but it raises an important point. Was Dinah a woman who was raped and about to be forced into a marriage against her will? Or was she a woman who loved someone her family disapproved of and paid a terrible price? We can never know for sure. Without the voice of the woman in the story being heard, we are only getting half the truth, which isn't truth at all.

Prayer

Heavenly Father, thank you that, through your Son, Jesus, you are not distant from the pain of your children. Our hearts cry out to you for all those who have experienced the pain and trauma of sexual violence. May they know the love and peace that surpasses all understanding. Amen

30

Tamar: ruin and righteousness

A bout three months later Judah was told, 'Your daughter-in-law Tamar has played the whore; moreover she is pregnant as a result of whoredom.' And Judah said, 'Bring her out, and let her be burned.' As she was being brought out, she sent word to her father-in-law, 'It was the owner of these who made me pregnant.' And she said, 'Take note, please, whose these are, the signet and the cord and the staff.' Then Judah acknowledged them and said, 'She is more in the right than I, since I did not give her to my son Shelah.' And he did not lie with her again.

GENESIS 38:24–26

There is a scene in the musical version of *Les Misérables* where Fantine, the young mother who had been ousted from her job and forced into prostitution to support her child, encounters the man who had been instrumental in her downfall, Jean

Valjean. Until that moment he had no idea what he had done, and when she confronted him, he had a choice as to how to react. He could deny all knowledge and go on his way, or he could choose the harder path of repentance. He chose the latter. There is a similar moment of realisation in the story of Tamar and Judah.

Like Fantine, Tamar didn't have much luck when it came to men. Her first husband was Er, the eldest son of Judah, one of Jacob's twelve sons. Er 'was wicked in the sight of the Lord' (Genesis 38:7) and died young. Levirite marriage laws decreed that the widow of a deceased man would be passed on to his brother. So Tamar was given in marriage to Judah's second son, Onan, in the hope that she would produce a child to continue Judah's clan, but Onan also died.

Tamar was then sent back to her father's household to wait for Judah's youngest son, Shelah, to come of age. Time went on, Shelah became an adult, and no marriage was arranged – it seemed that Tamar had been forgotten and was doomed to a life of poverty and social isolation. She decided to take matters into her own hands.

When she heard that Judah was going to be in nearby Timnah, she took off her widow's clothing, put on a veil and sat at the side of the road waiting for him to pass by. Judah noticed her but didn't recognise her and, taking her for a prostitute, propositioned her. She offered to sleep with him in return for a goat from his flock and then wisely asked for his ring (which would have contained a seal for signing contracts), the cord it hung on and his staff as a pledge. Judah had sex with her and then later sent his servant to seek her out to recover his belongings. By then Tamar was nowhere to be seen.

It is still sadly common for men to reveal double standards when it comes to sexual immorality, and Judah's reaction is a good example of this. Once he hears his daughter-in-law is pregnant, he demands that Tamar be dragged to the public square to burned. This was unusual, as although biblical laws had harsh punishments for sexual sin, there is no evidence in the Bible they were ever carried out. Tamar must have been terrified, but at the crucial moment she was able to produce the evidence that vindicated her. Like Jean Valjean, Judah had a choice to either deny and walk away or face up to what he had done. He chose the latter: 'Then Judah acknowledged them and said, "She is more in the right than I."'

Tamar had very little power over her life and was passed from man to man as property. This wasn't unusual; what is remarkable is that she took matters into her own hands and, in doing so, secured heirs and inserted herself into the familial line of Jesus himself (Matthew 1:3).

Reflection

Tamar's story reminds us of the occasion in John's gospel where a woman is similarly dragged before a gathered crowd and accused of sexual immorality. The religious leaders called for her to be stoned, but Jesus prevented this with these powerful words: 'Let anyone among you who is without sin be the first to throw a stone at her' (John 8:7).

It is so easy to judge others without knowing the full story, and the double standards that accuse women far more readily than men when it comes to sexual immorality are still prevalent.

Prayer

Wise and gracious God,
even in this fallen world where your life is distorted
you are revealed through acts of courage and compassion.
May we reject the temptations of self-indulgence
    and cowardice
and choose instead the costly way of truth.
Philippa White

⇒⇒ 31 ⇐⇐

Bathsheba: beauty and the beast

I t happened, late one afternoon, when David rose from his couch and was walking about on the roof of the king's house, that he saw from the roof a woman bathing; the woman was very beautiful. David sent someone to inquire about the woman. It was reported, 'This is Bathsheba daughter of Eliam, the wife of Uriah the Hittite.' So David sent messengers to fetch her, and she came to him, and he lay with her. (Now she was purifying herself after her period.) Then she returned to her house. The woman conceived; and she sent and told David, 'I am pregnant.'

2 SAMUEL 11:2–5

On 26 January 1998, President Bill Clinton stood alongside his wife and told the world, 'I did not have sexual relations with that woman, Miss Lewinski.' Almost every week we read of highly successful, respected leaders who claim to have 'strong moral principles' who yet seem to self-destruct at the peak of their careers by doing something unbelievably foolish which they know to be wrong and try to conceal. This has been termed 'Bathsheba Syndrome'.[9]

King David was around 50 years old when he first saw Bathsheba, almost the same age as Clinton. He too was a man at the pinnacle of his career: a charismatic leader who had worked his way from humble shepherd to king of all Israel; he had wealth, talent, loyal servants, a strong army and several wives.

It was late one afternoon in springtime, 'the time when kings go out to battle' (2 Samuel 11:1), and Bathsheba, the wife of Uriah (one of David's elite body-guards), was taking a customary bath to purify herself after her period. There is a common assumption that she was bathing publicly on the roof, hence arousing the ardour of the king; the Bible doesn't say this. In fact, it is David, who had made the fateful decision not to join his soldiers in battle, who was on the roof of his house. He spied her from afar and was so entranced by her beauty that he 'sent messengers to fetch her', slept with her and then returned her to her home.

News of Bathsheba's subsequent pregnancy set in motion a series of events which had tragic consequences. David, needing to cover up what he'd done, had Uriah brought back from battle and tried to entice him to have sex with his wife. Uriah, an honourable soldier through and through, refused to do this while his men were still in the middle of the battle: 'I will not do such a thing' (2 Samuel 11:11). In desperation, David sent word to his commander to put Uriah into the frontline of the battle and to withdraw protection from him 'so that he may be struck down and die' (2 Samuel 11:15). David's plan succeeded, making Bathsheba a widow and pregnant with the child of the man responsible for her husband's death, a child who went on to die young. David took her into his household as another wife.

Much has been written of David's subsequent grief, conviction of sin and public repentance, and we use his words, 'I have sinned against the Lord', in our confession prayer to this day (2 Samuel 12:13). We don't, however, know how Bathsheba felt: she isn't given any choice or voice in this part of her narrative. She does, however, have a chance to control the future of her son Solomon, the eldest of four further children she had with the king. Bathsheba is at David's death-bed when she helps to consolidate Solomon's succession to the throne, and she is named in the genealogy of Jesus: 'David was the father of Solomon by the wife of Uriah' (Matthew 1:6). Why is Uriah even mentioned here? Perhaps he is here as a reminder of David's fall from grace, and the need for a Saviour.

Reflection

Monica Lewinski, in a powerful TED talk entitled 'The price of shame', speaks about the personal consequences that the public humiliation following her affair with the president had on her and her family: 'I was branded as tramp, tart, slut, whore, bimbo, and, of course, "that woman". I was seen by many, but actually known by few. And I get it: it was easy to forget that that woman was dimensional, had a soul and was once unbroken.'[10]

The phrase 'it takes two to tango' is often bandied about when dealing with sexual matters, and in some situations this is quite right: women are not always vulnerable victims, as the story of Potiphar's wife reveals. The truth of the matter, though, is that it does not always take two to tango. Bathsheba did nothing to deserve David's treatment of her, and her story is sadly only too familiar today.

Prayer

Create in me a clean heart, O God, and put a new and right spirit within me. Do not cast me away from your presence, and do not take your holy spirit from me.
PSALM 51:10–11 *(David's prayer of repentance)*

32

Vashti: #MeToo

O n the seventh day, when the king was merry with wine, he commanded Mehuman, Biztha, Harbona, Bigtha and Abagtha, Zethar and Carkas, the seven eunuchs who attended him, to bring Queen Vashti before the king, wearing the royal crown, in order to show the peoples and the officials her beauty; for she was fair to behold. But Queen Vashti refused to come at the king's command conveyed by the eunuchs. At this the king was enraged, and his anger burned within him.

ESTHER 1:10–12

In October 2017 American actress Alyssa Milano posted on Twitter: 'If all the women who have been sexually harassed or assaulted wrote #MeToo as a status, we might give people a sense of the magnitude of the problem.' This was in response to allegations relating to renowned film producer Harvey Weinstein, who in February 2020 was sentenced to 23 years in prison. #MeToo became a global movement in a matter of days, opening up an important conversation about women's experiences, particularly in industries such as film and theatre. The story of Queen Vashti is perhaps one of the earliest accounts of a woman standing up to a powerful man.

Vashti was the queen of Persia, the first wife of King Ahasueres (Xerxes), and her story is told in the book of Esther during the days of Jewish captivity in Babylon. For the Persian rulers it was a time of peace and prosperity, which meant that there was plenty of time for the king to host banquets and display the glories of his kingdom. Ahasuerus was certainly a dedicated host – one of his parties was said to last nearly six months and was so lavish that there were couches made from gold and silver, drinks were served in golden goblets and the wine was so plentiful that 'each guest was allowed to drink without restriction' (Esther 1:8, NIV).

At that time the men and women of the royal palace lived largely separate lives, and Vashti had her own quarters. She was holding her own banquet for the women of the region when the drunken king, during one of his parties, demanded she be brought to him and displayed to the men, 'wearing the royal crown, in order to show the peoples and the officials her beauty.' Some argue that this meant the king demanded she should wear nothing at all but her crown! It's not clear if this is the case, but Vashti was clearly distressed by the command. She stood her ground and refused to go.

The king was furious and 'anger burned within him'. He had wanted to impress his guests with his wife's beauty, and instead she had humiliated him publicly. He wanted revenge. And so, like Henry VIII, Weinstein and countless other powerful men, he worked out a way to bring her down. He consulted his lawyers and they found a by-law which said he could depose her as queen for disobedience, which he did. This was good news for the nobles, who feared their own wives might hear about the queen's insubordination and become similarly disdainful of their husbands: 'There will be no end of contempt and wrath!' (Esther 1:18).

After Vashti was deposed a letter was sent throughout the whole land to every province, in every local language, with the decree that 'every man should be master in his own house' (Esther 1:22). The #MeToo movement was some way off!

Reflection

Women being harassed by drunken men at parties is nothing new, and standing up to a powerful man still comes at considerable cost, as Vashti found out. We don't get to hear why she did this. Some have argued that it was because of modesty (Midrash), others that she was unhappy with her appearance that day (Babylonian Talmud), and others say she was a proto-feminist fighting for her integrity.[11]

Let us pray for all those who continue to be exploited by the powerful, for all those who have the courage to stand up to power, and for ourselves, that we would use our own power well.

Prayer

Lord Jesus, who came into the world as one of us and
experienced what it is to be humiliated and shamed in front of others,
grant that those who carry the heavy burden of shame
might be released from its power over them;
and give us the confidence to speak boldly to rebuke vice
and proclaim your love. Amen

⤛ 33 ⤜

Susanna: completely trapped

W hen the maids had gone out, the two elders got up and ran to her. They said, 'Look, the garden doors are shut, and no one can see us. We are burning with desire for you; so give your consent, and lie with us. If you refuse, we will testify against you that a young man was with you, and this was why you sent your maids away.'

Susanna groaned and said, 'I am completely trapped. For if I do this, it will mean death for me; if I do not, I cannot escape your hands. I choose not to do it; I will fall into your hands, rather than sin in the sight of the Lord.'

Then Susanna cried out with a loud voice, and the two elders shouted against her.

SUSANNA 1:19–23

In March 2021 there was a letter in *The Times* newspaper from a young woman called Ella, aged 17. She wrote in response to the death of Sarah Everard, a woman killed by a stranger as she walked home. Sarah's death led to an outpouring of anger from women. Ella's letter eloquently explained why women were so angry. She wrote about all the times she'd experienced unwanted attention from men and expressed how difficult it is for women to know how to respond because 'each time a man harasses us in the street, we don't know where it will end'.

Susanna's story is found in the Greek, rather than the Hebrew, manuscripts of the book of Daniel (the Deuterocanonical portions of the Bible), so it is included as Daniel 13 in some Bibles and in the Apocrypha in others. She lived some time during the Babylonian exile, had been brought up to love the Lord and was married to a wealthy man called Joakim. They lived in an expensive house, which was also used as the main courthouse for the Jewish community, where the elders would gather to hear and pass judgement on all manner of offences.

Two of the community elders noticed Susanna's beauty and began 'to lust for her' (Susanna 8). Together they planned how they might find her on her own, and they took to hiding in her garden. One hot day Susanna was bathing alone there. The men ran over to her and demanded sex: 'Give your consent, and lie with us. If you refuse, we will testify against you that a young man was with you.'

Susanna knew instantly that she was in an impossible situation. There were two of them, she was naked, vulnerable and in an enclosed space, and as a woman she would never be believed. She said, 'I am completely trapped. For if I do this, it will mean death for me; if I do not, I cannot escape your hands.'

She shouted for help and so did her attackers, who then accused her of having sex with a man who had run off. She was taken in front of the assembly, unveiled in front of all the men and, without asking her for her side of the story or even considering the glaringly obvious plot holes in their story, she was found guilty of adultery and sentenced to death. Susanna's attackers were believed simply because 'they were elders of the people and judges' (Susanna 41).

Susanna cried out once again, this time in a prayer of desperation, 'O eternal God, you know what is secret… And now I am to die, though I have done none of the wicked things that they have charged against me!' (Susannah 43).

God heard her cries and stirred the conscience of Daniel, whose voice rose above the clamour of the mob: 'I want no part in shedding this woman's blood!' He challenged the assembly for being 'fools' and so quick to 'condemn a daughter of Israel without examination and without learning the facts' (Susannah 46–48). Daniel separated the two attackers and asked each of them to tell the court exactly where they had seen the couple being 'intimate with each other'. One of the men pointed to a small shrub and the other to an evergreen oak, and with this the men were revealed to have been lying. Susanna was spared, the men were put to death, and her family rejoiced because she was innocent after all.

Reflection

One of the slogans of the #MeToo movement is 'believe women', because the testimonies of women (and girls, men and boys, of course) who speak up about sexual harassment and abuse are still all too often ignored, disbelieved and silenced. Sadly this has been evident in the church as much as in the rest of society. Daniel refused to be influenced by the mob and paid attention to her words. In reality, many are still 'completely trapped' because of the fear that they won't be heard or believed, or they can't face reliving the trauma of their past. Our world, and our church, needs more Daniels.

Prayer

O Lord, hear; O Lord, forgive; O Lord, listen and act and do not delay! For your own sake, O my God, because your city and your people bear your name!
DANIEL 9:19

Women at work

In the traditional society of the Old Testament, women needed the protection of a husband and his family in order to be able to survive, and their work often involved looking after children, caring for the elderly and tending the sick. Some women were able to survive independently, but it was often a struggle. In this section we see some of the ways in which women used their skills to provide for themselves and their families. Some performed what has traditionally been considered as 'women's work' (Shiphrah and Puah, Rahab, Naaman's maidservant), others ran businesses (the medium of Endor, the Shunammite woman) and a few had jobs that are rather surprising (Abishag, the daughters of Shallum). What is clear for each one of them is that God used them in their work in all sorts of interesting ways.

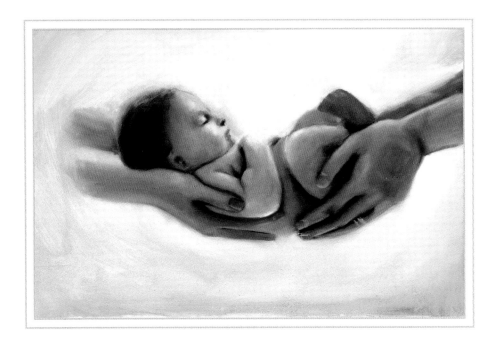

34

Shiphrah and Puah:
the rebel midwives

The king of Egypt said to the Hebrew midwives, one of whom was named Shiphrah and the other Puah, 'When you act as midwives to the Hebrew women, and see them on the birthstool, if it is a boy, kill him; but if it is a girl, she shall live.' But the midwives feared God; they did not do as the king of Egypt commanded them, but they let the boys live.

EXODUS 1:15–17

One of my favourite TV shows is *Call the Midwife*. Based on the memoirs of Jennifer Worth, the programme follows the life and work of a group of midwives who live in a religious order and work in east London after World War II. Each new life is brought into the world with a mixture of pain, struggle, endurance and joy. Sometimes it's pretty gruesome, but birth is like that. I've always admired midwives.

Having given birth three times, I know it's a messy business, and these women and men are willing to be at the gritty end. Midwives are the kind of people you want in a crisis: unflustered, clear thinking, plain talking, patient and encouraging. They are even willing to be shouted and sworn at in the course of their work!

Several midwives are mentioned in the Bible, but only two are mentioned by name. They are Shiphrah and Puah, two of the bravest women imaginable.

When Joseph worked as head of Pharaoh's household, the Jews and Egyptians worked together, experiencing a time of prosperity and wealth. This era was now over and the Pharaoh, believed to be Rameses II, felt threatened by the increasingly large Jewish population. He was afraid they would rise up against him and so he oppressed them, forcing them into conscripted labour and making 'their lives bitter with hard service' (Exodus 1:14). This didn't have the desired effect, and the Hebrew people continued to grow and thrive.

So Pharaoh, in his desperation, came up with a heinous plan to deprive the Israelites of leadership for generations to come. He summoned their midwives, including Shiphrah and Puah, and commanded them to murder all the male children at birth. In what is no doubt the first act of civil disobedience in recorded history, the midwives refused to follow this murderous edict: 'But the midwives feared

God; they did not do as the king of Egypt had commanded them, but they let the boys live.'

Pharaoh soon realised his orders had been ignored so he summoned Shiphrah and Puah to his palace to ask them why they had been disobedient. Telling the truth would have risked their livelihoods and perhaps even their lives. And so these brave women made up a racially charged explanation, one that would have been extremely hard for Pharaoh to disprove: 'The Hebrew women are not like the Egyptian women; they are vigorous and give birth before the midwife comes to them' (Exodus 1:19).

Ingenious. It seems that Pharaoh believed their explanation, and because of the cunning bravery of these women the Israelites continued to procreate, the boy babies lived, and Moses, who would later lead them into freedom, was born.

Reflection

There are still places in the world where babies are at risk because they are the 'wrong' gender or ethnicity. We are currently learning of the horrors of forced abortions and of the sterilisation of the Uighur people in China, and it is estimated that there are 130 million 'missing women' in the world due to selective abortion, mistreatment and neglect.[12]

Yet it was you who took me from the womb; you kept me safe on my mother's breast. On you I was cast from my birth, and since my mother bore me you have been my God.

PSALM 22:9–10

The imagery of a midwife is used by the psalmist to describe God drawing out new life and protecting and watching over her children. How beautiful to think of midwives, doctors, nurses and doulas, and all who attend women as they give birth, as being God-like in their work of bringing new life into the world.

Prayer

Creator God, who made the universe yet can number the very hairs on our head, as a midwife brings forth a new life into the world, you long to nurture new life in us today. Help us, your children, to trust in your love and protection, knowing that we are safe in your loving arms. Amen

❧ 35 ❧

Rahab: harlot, heroine or both?

The king of Jericho was told, 'Some Israelites have come here tonight to search out the land.' Then the king of Jericho sent orders to Rahab, 'Bring out the men who have come to you, who entered your house, for they have come only to search out the whole land.' But the woman took the two men and hid them. Then she said, 'True, the men came to me, but I did not know where they came from. And when it was time to close the gate at dark, the men went out. Where the men went I do not know. Pursue them quickly, for you can overtake them.' She had, however, brought them up to the roof and hidden them with the stalks of flax that she had laid out on the roof.

JOSHUA 2:2–6

Rahab is described as a harlot, or prostitute, and yet, despite her profession, and even though she wasn't born an Israelite, she is one of the few women named in the genealogy of Jesus at the beginning of Matthew's gospel. It's a story of woman who takes an enormous personal risk in order to protect her family and help the Israelite people.

Moses had died, and his assistant Joshua had taken over the leadership of the Israelites, who were still wandering in the wilderness. God had promised them that he would lead them into a fertile and abundant land, and they had camped in the Jordan valley opposite the city of Jericho in the hope that this was indeed the land they had been waiting for. But first they needed to check out the city and discern what likely opposition they would encounter. So Joshua sent two spies on a reconnaissance mission.

Rahab was a citizen of Jericho and she lived on the edges of the city, literally: 'Her house was on the outer side of the city wall and she resided within the wall itself' (Joshua 2:15). Joshua's spies went to stay at Rahab's house 'and spent the night there' (Joshua 2:1). We don't hear whether they were doing so because she had an inn or because of her other profession. It is likely, though, that this type of establishment would have been the ideal place for spies to gather intelligence, but that goes both ways and the king soon got wind of their presence.

When the king of Jericho he heard about the spies staying at Rahab's house, he ordered them to be brought to him. Rahab was cunning and, rather like the rebel midwives Shiphrah and Puah, defied the orders of her king to help the Israelites. She took them to the roof, hid them and sent the soldiers off in the wrong direction. She then made a pact with the spies: she would help them escape and in return they were to ensure that she and all her family would be unharmed when they eventually come to take the land. The pact was made, and the spies escaped.

Did Rahab act out of fear or faith, or purely to protect her family? She was certainly afraid of the power of the Israelites. She tells them, 'Dread of you has fallen on us, and that all the inhabitants of the land melt in fear before you' (Joshua 2:9). But she had also heard of the way in which God had led the people out of captivity and proclaimed, 'The Lord your God is indeed God' (Joshua 2:11). A little while later the city of Jericho was surrounded by the Israelites. They eventually took the city, but Rahab and all her family were spared and became incorporated into the Jewish people.

This book is not the place to debate the actions of the ancient people of Israel. Instead, let us focus on this remarkable woman who comes to be named in the New Testament as a hero of faith (Hebrews 11:31) and as an example of faith in action (James 2:25). She used her position, knowledge of people both within and outside of her culture, home, persuasive powers, charm and wily intellect to protect the Israelite spies and to secure the lives of her family, which would in time include Jesus of Nazareth. Rahab: harlot or heroine? Perhaps she was both.

Reflection

Jesus was criticised for spending time with those considered to be 'sinners' and 'unclean', such as prostitutes, tax collectors and lepers. Yet these 'sinners' were the first to recognise that he was the Saviour. Rahab's story reminds us that we too often make judgements about people because of their lifestyle, profession or values. God often chooses the most unlikely people to bring about his purposes.

Prayer

God of Rahab,
you call all people to acts of courage and compassion.
Teach us to hear your call through the needs around us,
and to respond with faith and action;
and remind us that nothing we have done
can ever put us out of the reach of your grace.

Philippa White

36

The medium of Endor: going the extra mile

So Saul disguised himself and put on other clothes and went there, he and two men with him. They came to the woman by night. And he said, 'Consult a spirit for me, and bring up for me the one whom I name to you.' The woman said to him, 'Surely you know what Saul has done, how he has cut off the mediums and the wizards from the land. Why then are you laying a snare for my life to bring about my death?' But Saul swore to her by the Lord, 'As the Lord lives, no punishment shall come upon you for this thing.' Then the woman said, 'Whom shall I bring up for you?' He answered, 'Bring up Samuel for me.'

1 SAMUEL 28:8–11

The next woman is commonly known as the witch of Endor, but she didn't practise magic: she was a medium, someone who consulted the dead. This was a common practice among many ancient religious traditions, but it was banned by Israelite law: 'Do not turn to mediums or wizards; do not seek them out' (Leviticus 19:31). Even though the practice was banned and, in theory, punishable by death, it seems that the medium of Endor had plenty of business and was well known by those seeking answers from beyond the grave.

One of these was King Saul, who in his desperation turned to one of the very people he had recently banished. He was preparing for what would turn out to be his final battle against the Philistine forces, who now had David on their side. Saul needed God's guidance, but this wasn't forthcoming and so, rather than prayerfully waiting on God, he disguised himself and went out late at night to see if a medium could consult the late prophet Samuel.

The medium of Endor let him in but was understandably wary. But she did what was asked of her and summoned the spirit of the prophet Samuel. There is much drama, such as you might expect from Madame Arcati in *Blithe Spirit*: 'She cried out with a loud voice… "I see a divine being coming up out of the ground"' (1 Samuel 28:12–13). At this point she saw through his disguise: 'Why have you deceived me? You are Saul!' (1 Samuel 28:12).

The spirit of Samuel told Saul what he didn't want to hear: that he had angered the Lord, and by the next day he and his sons would be dead. But the story ends with a gesture which shows the kindness and hospitality of a persecuted woman towards her oppressor. Seeing Saul's distress, she offered him food, persuaded him to stay and even killed the fatted calf and baked some bread. This was to be his last supper as he was indeed killed the very next day, alongside his sons.

Reflection

It's hard to know what to make of this story. Do we believe the soul of Samuel was really summoned up? Was this some kind of trickery, or the hallucination of a weary, hungry and desperate man? It's been a cause of debate for centuries, with the women being variously described as a ventriloquist, a demon and a prophet. She's been portrayed in fantasy art and even has a mention in the *Star Wars* franchise: the moon where the Ewoks live is called Endor. The Bible never says that contacting the dead is impossible, only that we are not to do it. That is clear enough for me.

But perhaps what is most striking about this story is the nature of the encounter between a woman who was part of a persecuted group and the very person who had banished her people. She did what was asked of her and went the extra mile, providing much-needed hospitality to her oppressor. An early good Samaritan, in fact!

Prayer

God beyond our understanding,
we give you thanks for those who listen for the needs of others
and who minister kindness and grace.
Give us the grace to forgive those who wrong us
and to be open to all we meet,
seeing in their faces your face of love.
Philippa White

37

Abishag the Shunammite: silent witness

K ing David was old and advanced in years; and although they covered him with clothes, he could not get warm. So his servants said to him, 'Let a young virgin be sought for my lord the king, and let her wait on the king, and be his attendant; let her lie in your bosom, so that my lord the king may be warm.' So they searched for a beautiful girl throughout all the territory of Israel, and found Abishag the Shunammite, and brought her to the king. The girl was very beautiful. She became the king's attendant and served him, but the king did not know her sexually.

1 KINGS 1:1–4

The weirdest job I've ever had was to remove ice barnacles from the feet of bantam chickens during a particularly freezing winter. Abishag the Shunammite had not only the best name in the Old Testament but also, arguably, the strangest job in the entire Bible. King David was by now 70 years old and very much past his prime. He was an infirm, weak old man, and was so unwell that he was cold all the time. His servants were worried for his life so they came up with a plan.

They went out and found Abishag, a beautiful young virgin girl who was probably only around twelve years old. She was brought to the palace to lie close to the king 'so that my lord the king may be warm'. She was essentially a human hot-water bottle! Thankfully the text clarifies that 'the king did not know her sexually', although this detail is probably added to emphasise David's weakness and frailty rather than to reassure us of Abishag's well-being.

Like any servant in a royal household, Abishag would have seen and heard a great deal from the sidelines. She was even in David's room to witness the drama of who would succeed him to the throne. The details of dynastic succession had not been worked out, but this did not deter Adonijah, David's eldest surviving son, from announcing himself king. He had support from a rogue priest called Abiathar, and they, perhaps prematurely as David had not yet died, held a large celebration banquet with numerous royal officials.

Years earlier David had promised the throne to his younger son, Solomon, whose mother was Bathsheba. A number of deathbed audiences ensued, with both Bathsheba and Nathan (the prophet who had earlier reprimanded David for sleeping with Bathsheba) pleading with the ailing king to take control of the situation. He eventually did: 'Your son Solomon shall succeed me as king, and he shall sit on my throne' (1 Kings 1:30). David died soon after and Solomon became king of Israel. Abishag witnessed everything from the edge of the room (1 Kings 1:15).

A little while later the ousted prince Adonijah returned to the palace and pleaded with Bathsheba for the hand of Abishag in marriage. Bathsheba took the request to Solomon, who was furious: 'And why do you ask Abishag the Shunammite for Adonijah? Ask for him the kingdom as well!' (1 Kings 2:22). Why was he so angry? It's likely that Solomon realised that Adonijah's proposal was a last-ditch attempt to obtain the throne. This reveals that Abishag was considered part of David's harem, and therefore a marriage to her would have been politically expedient. It backfired badly, as Solomon was so enraged that he had Adonijah killed and Abiathar removed from the priesthood.

Abishag doesn't speak at all in the Bible narrative; she is a silent servant on the fringes of a power struggle, and we don't know what happened to her after David's death. It is likely that she remained part of Solomon's extensive harem.

Reflection

It's hard for us to imagine a role like the one given to Abishag the Shunammite as ever being acceptable, but it was not unusual for younger people to lie close to elderly people to transfer their natural body heat. As we reflect on Abishag's story, let's remember in prayer all who care for the elderly and those at the end of their lives, particularly nurses, home carers and those who work in hospitals and hospices and nursing homes.

Prayer

God of Abishag,
we give you thanks that nobody is insignificant to you.
Have mercy on all those who are treated as objects,
valued only for their usefulness,
whose humanity is forgotten.
May we work for a world
where all human beings are valued as your children,
the young, old and vulnerable are protected,
and all have a voice.
Philippa White

38

The Shunammite woman: a rising hope

When the man of God saw her coming, he said to Gehazi his servant, 'Look, there is the Shunammite woman; run at once to meet her, and say to her, Are you all right? Is your husband all right? Is the child all right?' She answered, 'It is all right.' When she came to the man of God at the mountain, she caught hold of his feet. Gehazi approached to push her away. But the man of God said, 'Let her alone, for she is in bitter distress; the Lord has hidden it from me and has not told me.' Then she said, 'Did I ask my lord for a son? Did I not say, Do not mislead me?'

2 KINGS 4:25b–28

Often the unnamed women in the Bible are poor, on the edges of society and only sketchily described. The 'Shunammite woman', on the other hand, was wealthy, well known and one of the most remarkable women in this series, particularly when contrasted with her weak and indecisive husband.

The childless couple lived in the village of Shunem, where the prophet Elisha was based. The woman was an enthusiastic host, and Elisha and his servant Gehazi would drop in for a meal whenever they passed through. Over time, they did this so often that the woman suggested that they create a guest room for them. She was clearly a woman with an eye for detail, and the room was lovingly furnished with 'a bed, a table, a chair, and a lamp' (2 Kings 4:10). A few years later this little upper room would be the location of one of the prophet Elisha's greatest miracles.

Elisha and Gehazi wanted to give something back to the woman in return for her hospitality and kindness. They knew that as she was childless and her husband elderly, there would be no one to look after her when he died. Unlike Sarai and Hannah, this woman never asked for a child, but the prophet tells her that she would be pregnant by the following year, which she was.

Despite this miracle birth, several years later disaster struck. The young boy became seriously ill while in the fields with his father. He cried out for help, 'Oh, my head, my head!' (2 Kings 4:19). The father, either unable or unwilling to carry the boy himself, got a servant to take him to his wife, whereupon the boy died in her arms.

She immediately sprang into action. She took the child upstairs to Elisha's room, laid him on the bed, shut the door and then made the 50-kilometre round trip to Mount Carmel to find Elisha. Her husband was of no help at all and only muttered something about it not being the right day to visit a prophet. When she got there, she refused to speak to the servant Gehazi and went directly to Elisha, where she gave him a piece of her mind: 'Did I ask my Lord for a son? Did I not say, Do not mislead me?'

The woman insisted that Elisha come immediately and, after initially trying to suggest his servant go in his place, Elisha relented. Once at the house, Elisha went to the little room and prayed to the Lord. His method of healing was both physical and dramatic. The prophet 'lay upon the child, putting his mouth upon his mouth, his eyes upon his eyes, and his hands upon his hands' (2 Kings 4:34). After Elisha did this twice, the boy sneezed and returned to life.

The boy's resurrection compelled the woman to fall to her knees in praise and thanksgiving.

Reflection

Writer Mirabai Starr likens her grief after the death of her daughter to an 'abyss… an avalanche, annihilating everything in its path'. In those early moments of grief, the Shunammite woman lashed out in anger. Stories of resurrection and hope like this one become more prevalent towards the end of the Hebrew scriptures as the messianic age of Jesus Christ draws closer. Elijah and Elisha's healing miracles were a foretaste of what was to come, and there are clear echoes between this story and the healing of the son of the widow of Nain in Luke 7:11–17.

Of course, most children who die are not miraculously healed, and most grieving mothers are not reunited with their children in this life. However, this story reminds us of the hope of the resurrection, which is revealed through Jesus Christ, who raised the dead, was himself raised and promises that we too will be raised up.

Prayer

May the cry of widows, orphans and destitute children enter into thine ear, O most loving Saviour. Comfort them with a mother's tenderness, shield them from the perils of this world, and bring them at last to thy heavenly home.

John Cosin (1594–1672)

39

Naaman's maidservant: brave advice

Naaman, commander of the army of the king of Aram, was a great man and in high favour with his master, because by him the Lord had given victory to Aram. The man, though a mighty warrior, suffered from leprosy. Now the Arameans on one of their raids had taken a young girl captive from the land of Israel, and she served Naaman's wife. She said to her mistress, 'If only my lord were with the prophet who is in Samaria! He would cure him of his leprosy.' So Naaman went in and told his lord just what the girl from the land of Israel had said. And the king of Aram said, 'Go then, and I will send along a letter to the king of Israel.'

2 KINGS 5:1–5a

This next story involves a contagious disease known as leprosy. Those suffering from this illness were designated 'unclean' and were separated from society for the protection of others. The Covid-19 pandemic has shown us all too clearly how terrifying a contagious disease can be and the indiscriminate way in which it can infect people from all walks of life.

Leprosy had infected Naaman, the powerful commander of the king of Aram's army, and his healing came through the brave words of a young, unnamed servant girl. Naaman's maidservant was a young Israelite, probably around twelve years old, who had been captured during one of the many raids on Israel by their Aramean enemies in the north. She had been given as a servant to Naaman's wife.

Despite the turbulent situation in Israel at the time, there was still a remnant who worshipped the true and living God (1 Kings 19:18). It is likely that our servant girl came from one of these families. Perhaps this enabled her to speak up when she saw Naaman's distress: 'She said to her mistress, "If only my lord were with the prophet who is in Samaria! He would cure him of his leprosy."'

While we can't begin to fathom the circumstances, we can imagine the terror that this young girl would have felt when she was captured in an armed raid. Taken to a foreign land to work as a slave, surely she must have resented her captors for ripping her away from her family and homeland. Did she also secretly enjoy watching her master suffer from his painful and debilitating skin disease?

We cannot know how she felt, but what we do know is the choice that she made. She sought to help him by pointing him towards someone whom she knew had the power to heal: the prophet Elisha. It is extraordinary that these few confident, faithful words from a servant girl had such power that they galvanised the whole family into action.

They travelled to Israel to seek an audience with Elisha. We don't know if Naaman took his wife and servant girl with him, but it is likely he did. What must it have been like for her to travel back to her homeland, a place where she was once free and loved, but this time with those who had captured her and killed her people?

I wonder if she witnessed Elisha the prophet, who, to Naaman's horror, sent out his servant to tell him that his healing would only come if he washed himself in the river Jordan seven times. Did she witness him being healed, not just of his skin condition, but also of his arrogance, pride and self-importance? Was she worried whether those confident words which sparked such a journey would be fulfilled? What if Naaman didn't get healed by Elisha and the whole journey was in vain? What would be the consequences of this for her?

Any fears would have been assuaged when Naaman eventually 'immersed himself seven times in the Jordan... his flesh was restored like the flesh of a young boy, and he was clean' (2 Kings 5:14).

Reflection

The story of this faithful servant girl is a reminder of the importance of having the courage to speak up about our faith, especially when this might help someone in need. How often have we been by the side of someone who is sick or in need of guidance and we've held our tongue? How often have we kept quiet about our faith in case we are ridiculed, mocked or ignored? Are there moments in your own life when you wish you had spoken up? Let us pray for the courage and faith of this young girl in our own lives.

Prayer

Almighty God, bestow upon us the meaning of words, the light of understanding, the nobility of diction and the faith of the true nature. And grant us that what we believe we may also speak.

Hilary of Poitiers (c. 315–67)

40

Shallum's daughters: let us rebuild

Next to them Jedaiah son of Harumaph made repairs opposite his house; and next to him Hattush son of Hashabneiah made repairs. Malchijah son of Harim and Hasshub son of Pahath-moab repaired another section and the Tower of the Ovens. Next to him Shallum son of Hallohesh, ruler of half the district of Jerusalem, made repairs, he and his daughters.

NEHEMIAH 3:10–12

In February 2011 a massive earthquake struck Christchurch, New Zealand, causing destruction to the city. Much of the city centre, including homes, schools and its cathedral, was decimated. In the aftermath a student called Sam Johnson used Facebook to rally a student volunteer army, which became a collective movement of over 2,000 young people. Together they went to work shovelling rubble out of homes, distributing supplies and supporting the community. It was a remarkable example of what is possible when people come together.

The final women in this book share only a glancing mention in one single verse in the last book of the historical narrative of the Hebrew Bible. Shallum's daughters helped repair a little section of a ruined wall, so why are they worth mentioning? In order to understand this, it is helpful to know the significance of what they were helping to rebuild.

When Judah was invaded by the Babylonians (see chapter on Huldah), the city of Jerusalem was destroyed, including its palaces, the holy temple and the grand city walls. The Jewish people were cast out and for nearly a century had lived in exile and were only given permission to return when King Cyrus of Persia came to the throne. There was a huge amount of restoration to do. They needed to rebuild the house of God, restore the holiness and purity of the Jewish people, and then secure the city itself by rebuilding the walls. Much of the work of the first two stages is recounted in the book of Ezra.

A young cup-bearer named Nehemiah was called by God to oversee this final building project: 'Jerusalem lies in ruins with its gates burnt. Come, let us rebuild' (Nehemiah 2:17). Realising the enormity of the task, Nehemiah, rather like Sam

Johnson, inspired the whole community to get to work. Each family was to take a section of the wall, from the Sheep Gate in the north to the Fish Gate in the west and the Dung Gate in the south. Nehemiah 3 details every family by name, noting that only 'their nobles would not put their shoulders to the work' (Nehemiah 3:5).

The daughters of Shallum are the only women named in the rebuilding work. I find it intriguing to wonder what their role involved and how exactly they helped their father. Perhaps they financed the work or brought food and drink to the labourers. Or did they do actual hard labour, carrying stones, placing beams, hoisting doors and shovelling rubble? Whatever their exact role, they were part of the working party who finished the wall in only 52 days, enabling the Jewish families to return home (Nehemiah 7) to live and worship in safety.

Reflection

The daughters of Shallum helped to build the walls in Jerusalem that were still standing during Jesus' final journey into the city. He may even have ridden through the gate they built when he arrived on the colt. Or perhaps he passed their section of the wall when he was being dragged towards the cross on his final journey where his body (which he compared to the temple) was destroyed before it was restored in all its resurrected glory.

The Covid-19 pandemic was a kind of 'earthquake' in the world, as many of the structures that we thought of as strong and solid turned out to be weaker than we ever imagined, and many people felt their world crumbling around them. There is still much rebuilding to be done. Like the daughters of Shallum, each one of us is called to play our own little part in the rebuilding work of God's kingdom, a kingdom that can never be destroyed and will last forever.

Prayer

God of hard work and healing,
as we remember those who have laboured on behalf of your people
and rebuilt your church in every generation,
may we take our part in your work of renewal
and build in our communities
bridges for healing, homes for rest,
and churches where you come to dwell among your people.
Philippa White

Reflection on the artwork process: Micah Hayns

What is your background in art?

I have been visually creative since I was very young. I began drawing cartoons and slowly gravitated towards portraiture and more realistic scenes as I grew older. My desire to learn the traditional craft of drawing and painting brought me to the Florence Academy of Art, Italy, where I spent a year rigorously studying the drawing techniques of the Old Masters, such as Michelangelo and Leonardo. I also love more contemporary styles, such as pop art, abstract expressionism and collage, and I often try to harmonise and balance both traditional and modern techniques in my work.

What inspired you to take on this project?

I am passionate about promoting equality in the church and so the opportunity to use my craft to amplify some of the inspiring stories of women in the Old Testament, who often get overlooked, was very exciting. As an artist who is also a Christian, the chance to capture and honour how God has moved and worked in people within the biblical stories is important for me and my faith.

What were the challenges of illustrating the book?

Firstly, 40 images is a lot! So I had to dig deep to find the perseverance and stamina to get through them all. I had to make each one unique and reflect the character, story and essence of the woman and so I used a lot of different tools and techniques to try to capture each one. Although there are just 40, I probably made over 80, half of which I didn't take forward. For example, I made four versions of Sarah before I was happy!

What is your hope for the book?

My hope is that my pictures connect and bring meaning and light to the stories. Ultimately if people feel closer to God in some way or receive a sense of life or peace from my pictures and my mum's writing, then I feel we have done our job.

Find Micah online:

Website: **micahhayns.com**
Facebook/Instagram: **@micahhaynsart**

Notes

1 'Bradwell v. Illinois', 83 US 130 (1872), quoted in a speech by Lady Brenda Hale, '100 years of women in the law: from Bertha Cave to Brenda Hale', 20 March 2019.

2 'Report of the Advisory Panel on Judicial Diversity', chaired by Baroness Neuberger, February 2010, p. 4, accessible at **judiciary.uk**.

3 Goal 5 of the UN's Sustainable Development Goals is: 'achieve gender equality and empower all women and girls', and sub-goal 5.a states: 'Undertake reforms to give women equal rights to economic resources, as well as access to ownership and control over land and other forms of property, financial services, inheritance and natural resources, in accordance with national laws', **sdgs.un.org/goals/goal5**.

4 William McDonald, *The Socialite Who Killed a Nazi with Her Bare Hands* (Workman, 2012).

5 Paul Vitello, 'Nancy Wake, proud spy and Nazi foe, dies at 98', *The New York Times*, 13 August 2011, **nytimes.com/2011/08/14/world/europe/14wake.html**.

6 Christine de Pizan, *The Treasure of the City of Ladies*, translated by Sarah Lawson (Penguin, 1985).

7 The son was named either Chileab (2 Samuel 3:3) or Daniel (1 Chronicles 3:1).

8   'Emily' was the pseudonym given to Chanel Miller, who has now written a book of her experience called *Know My Name: A memoir* (Penguin, 2019). Her victim impact statement is readily available online, as it was shared 11 million times in four days once it was released on Buzzfeed.

9   The term was coined in a fascinating article: Dean C. Ludwig and Clinton O. Longenecker, 'The Bathsheba Syndrome: the ethical failure of successful leaders', *Journal of Business Ethics*, 12 (1993), pp. 265–73.

10   **ted.com/talks/monica_lewinsky_the_price_of_shame**

11   **myjewishlearning.com/article/vashti-esther-a-feminist-perspective**

12   Hannah Richie and Max Roser, 'Gender ratio' (June 2019): **ourworldindata.org/gender-ratio**

Enabling all ages to grow in faith

Anna Chaplaincy

Living Faith

Messy Church

Parenting for Faith

BRF is a Christian charity that resources individuals and churches. Our vision is to enable people of all ages to grow in faith and understanding of the Bible and to see more people equipped to exercise their gifts in leadership and ministry.

To find out more about our work, visit
brf.org.uk